The Wolves of Isle Royale

By Rolf O. Peterson

The Wolves of Isle Royale

A Broken Balance

WILLOW CREEK PRESS
Minocqua, Wisconsin

Dedication

For my wife, Candy, and our sons,
Jeremy and Trevor, for whom the magic
of Isle Royale will last a lifetime.

ISBN 1-57223-031-2

Published by WILLOW CREEK PRESS, P.O. Box 147, Minocqua, WI 54548
For information on other Willow Creek titles, write or call 1-800-850-WILD.

Designed by Patricia Bickner Linder
Edited by Greg Linder

Library of Congress Cataloging-in-Publication Data

Peterson, Rolf O.
    The wolves of Isle Royale : a broken balance / by Rolf O. Peterson.
        p.   cm.
    ISBN 1-57223-031-2 (alk. paper)
    1. Wolves—Michigan—Isle Royale National Park. 2. Moose—Michigan—
Isle Royale National Park. 3. Predation (Biology) 4. Animal communities—
Michigan—Isle Royale National Park. 5. Isle Royale National Park (Mich.)
I. Title.
QL737.C22P475   1995
599.74'442—dc20   95-35263
                                                   CIP

Printed in the United States.

Contents

Preface

IT HAS BEEN LESS THAN A CENTURY SINCE SCIENTISTS
first set foot on Isle Royale, then a remote and wild
island in Lake Superior, now, in addition, a U.S.
national park. The immensity of Lake Superior, more
than anything else, has defined for human observers
the character of Isle Royale.

It is the lake that has influenced its climate and
restricted the flow of life from the mainland to the
island, including visits by scientists. If Louis Aggasiz,
the most celebrated American scientist of his
generation, had been able to travel to Isle Royale in the
1850s as planned, the scientific payoff might have been
handsome. Aggasiz's trip to the island by small boat,
powered by wind and oar, was canceled by a storm.
Science, like life itself, is a contingent affair, always
building on the past and extending unpredictably into
the future.

The past at Isle Royale now includes a rich legacy
of scientific discoveries about the natural world. In the
half century that gray wolves have inhabited Isle
Royale, the monitoring of their numbers and
interpretation of their ecology have become annual
quests. Public attitudes about this great carnivore have
been transformed and to this end Isle Royale has
played a role that has been of worldwide significance.

I have tried to portray for general readers what we
know about a chronic decline in Isle Royale wolves
that began in the 1980s. Our current understanding
of the problem is woven into chapters that take the
reader through the seasons on this island, for the
changing seasons are the most important context for

The author with his family in front of Bangsund Cabin in 1982.

life on Isle Royale. Seasons also define what scientists actually do on the ground to understand the dynamics of wolves and moose.

This book provides what science generally has little room for in the straitjacket format of its formal literature—those "single, startling incidents of animal behavior" mentioned by Barry Lopez. These were memorable incidents, all of them, direct observations that have left me humored, perplexed, gratified, or in wonder. This is the raw material of direct observation. For me, there could be no greater source of inspiration than nature itself.

Today no one questions the immense value of wolves on Isle Royale, where this predator enjoys more security from human avarice than do wolves anywhere else on the planet. Much has been learned simply by long-term observations at Isle Royale. Will this approach suffice in the future, or should humans actively chart a course for this wilderness island? These are questions pondered in this book.

—Rolf O. Peterson

Acknowledgments

I AM DEEPLY INDEBTED TO MANY PEOPLE FOR MAKING this book a reality. My wife, Candy, patiently and thoroughly worked on the text time and time again, in what must have been a labor of love. For playing instrumental roles in the actual work, I will gratefully highlight the contributions of Durward Allen, Don Murray, and Don Glaser. Literally hundreds of people contributed directly to the field work, and I thank each of them for their personal contribution.

Prominent long-term funding for the research was provided by the following: Isle Royale National Park, National Science Foundation, Earthwatch, National Geographic Society, Boone and Crockett Club, and Robert Bateman/Mill Pond Press. Many other organizations and individuals have also assisted and tax-deductible donations are gladly accepted by "Wolf-moose fund", Michigan Tech Fund, Alumni House, Michigan Technological University, Houghton, MI 49931.

The following individuals offered helpful comments on portions of the book: Durward Allen, Elizabeth Amberg, Peter Armington, Douglas Barnard, Tim and Jean Cochrane, William Fink, David Harmon, Robert Krumenaker, Terry Lindsay, Robert Linn, L. David Mech, Jack Oelfke, and Ami Walsh. At Willow Creek Press, Tom Petrie, Pat Linder and Greg Linder all made the final task of production an enjoyable one.

Foreword

THE WOLF IS IN THE PUBLIC EYE. RED WOLVES HAVE been reintroduced into the southeastern U.S. and gray wolves into Yellowstone and Idaho. Natural wolf packs have repopulated Wisconsin, Michigan, and Montana. Some 2,000 wolves now inhabit Minnesota and are overflowing into North and South Dakota. A direct beneficiary of the Endangered Species Act, the wolf is making a comeback.

Before any of this took place, however, wolves found their way some 15-20 miles across the Lake Superior ice from Ontario to Isle Royale National Park. In 1949 that 210-square-mile gem of an island was ideal for wolves. It supported a moose herd that for half a century had never felt the fang of a wolf. The right combination of wandering mainland wolves and a solid ice bridge to the island apparently only happened once.

The Isle Royale wolves flourished, and so did the moose. And so did scientists who followed both populations. The island was an ideal natural laboratory in which to count the wolves and the moose and to study their interactions over time. Durward Allen of Purdue University spawned the idea and gathered the funds. He charged me with getting the project started, and I spent four years doing so in pursuit of my Ph.D.

Several other graduate students and post-doctoral fellows followed, entranced by the island's pristine nature, intrigued by the mysteries of its moose-wolf system, and rewarded by the troves of data they added to the unique story.

One of those students was Rolf Peterson, who

showed up in the early 1970s. Rolf came to earn his Ph.D. like several of his predecessors. But by then Durward Allen, the dean of the project, was retiring and looking for someone well suited to whom to hand off the study for good. Rolf Peterson fit the bill.

Not only did Rolf conduct his Ph.D. work, but he also summarized and synthesized the data from all the previous workers. He then went on to continue the project in the same vein. A whole new series of graduate students under Rolf's direction carry the torch to this day.

Meanwhile, the wolves and moose of Isle Royale continued doing what they damn well pleased. For some periods, their interactions became predictable. But conditions changed, and new predictions emerged. Some have stood long tests of time, others shorter. And some events on Isle Royale have defied explanation. From 1980 when the wolves peaked at 50, they plummeted to 14 in 1982. After a decade and a half more, their numbers have not recovered to even half their former peak.

As scientists around the world eagerly await the annual reports of Isle Royale's current wolf and moose numbers, Peterson and his team work assiduously to try both to get them and to explain them. The quest continues.

Did canine parvovirus cause the steep decline in the early 1980s? Does inbreeding depression explain the population's recent stagnation? Or are these extreme population behaviors the results merely of random influences on a tiny population lacking the usual buffering mechanisms of larger ones?

After all, who could argue that 30 years of close inbreeding hurt the population when wolf numbers rose from the basic pair that must have settled the island about 1949 to 50 animals in 1980? If 30 years of inbreeding did not hurt the wolf population, did 31? Perhaps. But not necessarily. The truth is, we really do not know.

Rolf Peterson aims to find out, however, whatever it takes. And he should. This longest-studied wolf-moose system is, to my knowledge, the longest-studied population of vertebrates, possibly of any organism, ever. Science has a major stake in the findings.

Of course, this grand experiment may be over any year. If inbreeding depression is affecting the population, things will not improve as time goes on. Or if wolf numbers remain low (16 in 1995), various chance events might bring their demise.

Rolf agonizes over all of this. After tracing the wolf-moose story on Isle Royale and describing his most interesting personal adventures ferreting out the details in a very readable fashion, he turns philosophic. Isle Royale is a national park. One of the mandates of national parks is to preserve their natural ecosystems. What if the Isle Royale wolves become extinct? Should the National Park Service replace them?

This is not an easy question to answer, and Rolf explores the dilemmas involved. Much of the issue turns on the degree to which the wolf-moose system and any causes of its disruption are construed as "natural." But Rolf maintains that "naturalness" is an elusive, relative term and that there may be higher values involved than merely adhering rigidly to what might be considered an arbitrary, vague standard of "naturalness." His discussion of the subject is enough to make you think.

Meanwhile, I am betting on the wolves to get us out of all this. The Isle Royale population has come through thick and thin, and some deleterious genes may have been cleansed from it in the process. It has recently produced a spate of young, probably poised soon for reproduction.

The island's moose and beavers, squirrels and hares, and all the rest of its mammals are also isolated and must also be highly inbred. They have been doing fine for decades or even centuries. Admittedly, the wolves' naturally lower numbers place them in greater jeopardy. Thus I will not really be surprised if they fall first. But neither will I be surprised if they hang on for decades more.

In any case, Rolf Peterson's treatise here will serve us well either by laying out the thinking behind any wolf reintroduction that may take place or by colorfully documenting the history of a population that almost needed one. Only time will tell.

—L. David Mech

Thunder Bay,
Ontario

ISLE ROYALE

LAKE SUPERIOR

Houghton, Michigan

Duluth, Minnesota

Sault Ste. Marie

LITTLE
TODD H.

Hatchet

L. Desor

Mud L.

Little Siskiwit R.

Hay Bay

SISKIWIT BAY

N
W   E
S

McGinty Cove

Beaver I.   ● Windigo

Thompson I.

Johns I.

Pt. Houghton

WASHINGTON HARBOR

Washington I.

GRACE HARBOR

Big Siskiwit River

L. Halloran

Cumberland Pt.

Feldtman L.

Feldtman Ridge.

Rainbow Cove

Passage Island

Blake Point

Five Finger Bay
Duncan Bay
Edwards I.

Amygdaloid Island
AMYGDALOID HARBOR
Belle Isle
Robinson Bay
TOBIN HARBOR
Shaw I. Raspberry I.
ROCK HARBOR

Lake Eva
Mt. Franklin +

McCargoe Cove
Linklater L.
+ Mt. Ojibway
Mott Island

Sargent L.
Daisy Farm
campground
E. Caribou I.
W. Caribou I.

Beaver L. McDonald L.
Anglewom L.
Bangsund summer
research cabin

Otter L.
Chickenbone L.
Moskey
Basin

RBOR

L.
LeSage

L. Harvey + Mt. Siskiwit
L. Richie

Intermediate
L.
Chippewa
Harbor

L. Whittlesey

Siskiwit Lake

Malone Bay

ght I.

Long I.

Isle Royale National Park

This 1755 map of "New France" or "Canada" was used in negotiations behind the Treaty of Paris in 1785, when the boundary between the U.S. and Canada was established. For over 75 years, "Isle Philippeaux" or "Isle Minong" existed on maps alongside "Isle Royale," but one of these large islands was ficticious.

The Living Laboratory

On this continent and in the world, Isle Royale is an almost unique repository of primitive conditions. Like a priceless antique, it will be even more valuable in times not far ahead.

Durward L. Allen, *Wolves of Minong,* 1979

IN 1755 A MAP OF LAKE SUPERIOR WAS PUBLISHED THAT had been meticulously assembled from shoreline surveys. Seeing this map brings to mind the fable about the ten blind men who described an elephant, each with access to a different part of the creature. In the 1755 map several large islands were erroneously charted in Lake Superior, probably noted by observers on opposite shores. In reality, only one large island exists in Lake Superior, an island called *Minong* by Native Americans (meaning "place of blueberries" or "a nice place to be"), and named Isle Royale by early French explorers.

Mapmakers are not alone in their subjective perspectives on Isle Royale. Some adventurous souls braved the unpredictable waters of Lake Superior to seek their fortunes in copper, fish, furs, or timber. More recently, people have sought refuge on Isle Royale, finding that solitude and adventure is an effective antidote to the allergens and rat race of the mainland.

Scholars have also been intrigued by the island; the human brain seems compelled to probe and understand the earth and its creatures. Yet even scholars view Isle Royale with varied perspectives. Whereas cultural historians are fascinated by the steady procession of people to the island, natural scientists have valued the island's geological, botanical, and zoological features.

For ecologists, the island has been viewed as a natural system simple enough to be understood, even predictable to a degree, yet large enough to be instructive as a microcosm, or a smaller version of the world. Like the explorers and mapmakers before them, ecologists found a challenge on Isle Royale, for even as they filled in the details and their models became more accurate, they realized they were tracking a moving target. Physical features of the earth are rather static, so a mapmaker can reasonably hope to get it right; but nature is a dynamic play with shifting scenery and unpredictable actors. At Isle Royale any ten-year interval, if examined closely, would yield vastly different conclusions about what is actually happening.

The story of Isle Royale's wildlife is familiar to many who have never set foot on the island. I am told that every Norwegian child learns the story of Isle Royale's wolves and moose in elementary school. Since 1958 the dramatic interaction between the island's wolves, moose, and forests has been studied to understand animal abundance in a place where humans give nature free rein. In this book I present a wildlife ecologist's perspective, forged after two decades of tramping over the ground and thousands of hours of observation from small aircraft. As both a comprehensive introduction and a useful summary, this book carries my hope that Isle Royale will continue to be a place of discovery and inspiration.

*   *   *

Although Isle Royale's isolation and remoteness make work difficult for scientists, the island also has qualities that make it an attractive study area. Due to its limited collection of animal species (most have simply never arrived) and its protection from meddling by "modern man," the island is an ideal natural laboratory.

Of the four dozen or so species of mammals found on the adjacent Ontario shore, only 15 reached Isle Royale and remain today. Fortunately, the present cast includes species that play pivotal roles in the boreal forest—wolves, moose, beavers, foxes, and snowshoe hares. There are no deer or caribou to compete with the moose, tempt the wolves, or complicate the picture for scientists. Gray wolves are the only large predators, and they have no competition from humans or bears.

Another ideal feature of Isle Royale as a laboratory is the natural fence provided by the frigid ice water of Lake Superior. We can usually count the island's wolves and moose each year and know that all change is due to births and deaths—the basic arithmetic is simple.

Finally, geographic isolation provides better security for wolves than does regulation. Ludwig Carbyn, a Canadian wolf biologist, believes that there may not be a single wolf pack in Canada—even in national parks—that is not vulnerable to human-caused mortality. This is almost certainly true for Russia, the other stronghold of the world's wolves. In Minnesota, where almost 2,000 wolves are fully protected by law and persist on the edge of their Canadian range, wolf expert L. David Mech suspects that 50 percent of wolf mortality may be due to humans. People hit wolves with their vehicles, shoot at them indiscriminately, and illegally take them in traps and snares. If one were to look throughout the world for a bounded, discrete population of wild wolves that is free of threat from humans, the search would begin and end at Isle Royale.

*   *   *

Careful excavations by National Park Service (NPS) archaeologists have revealed evidence of early human encampments. Humans have been part of the Isle Royale scene for at least 4,000 years, when the earliest copper diggings were made. Prehistoric evidence and early records show that Native Americans knew Isle Royale well as a place to hunt, fish, and mine pure copper in summer expeditions from the north shore of Lake Superior. Stone flakes, bits of pottery, bones of fish, and occasionally bones of beaver and caribou have been found on virtually every beach on Isle Royale, but no trace of ancient moose. The absence of moose at Isle Royale prior to the present century may be related to the Native American way of life that prevailed on the mainland before the European invasion. Moose often stand their ground to defend themselves from wolves, but this behavior made them highly vulnerable to humans armed with spears or

Sunset over a calm Lake Superior belies the treachery that has led to several shipwrecks off this point at the west end of Isle Royale. (Cumberland Point)

Lake Superior generates its own weather, including fog and cold in summer and here, lake-effect snow in winter, as vapor from a cloud bank is transformed directly into snow.

bows and arrows—especially if dogs were along to help. Later, rifles made the hunt even more efficient.

Isle Royale is a single day's paddle from Grand Portage, the center of the North American fur trade of the 18th and 19th centuries. Given the number of people nearby who were bent on exploiting wildlife during the period, the absence of moose during this period is not in the least mysterious. After persisting for thousands of years, the economy of Native Americans finally collapsed as European encroachment drove them from their traditional homelands.

A century ago, hundreds of people in bustling communities attempted to wrest a profit from veins of copper coursing through the layered basalts that form the backbone of Isle Royale. Now-extinct passenger pigeons were shot from their roosts for food and sport, and enormous lake sturgeon were netted in the island's harbors for commercial trade. After a century of hunting with firearms, only a remnant woodland caribou population was left. Beaver, the trappers' currency, had already become rare. Bullets and traps brought to Isle Royale the same destruction of wildlife that prevailed throughout North America in the 19th century.

As European settlement proceeded, the giant pine forests of the Great Lakes states were cut, and the remaining slash was consumed by wildfires. Simultaneously, hopes of high profits attracted a frenzied rush of miners to extract mineral wealth. Isolation and difficult working conditions at Isle Royale precluded lumbering and mining on a grand scale, but mineral seekers set fires in the 19th century to expose the copper-bearing basalt flows on the eastern end of the island, where only thin soils had accumulated since the glaciers had retreated.

Today, after a century of forest recovery, the old stands of birch and aspen that followed on the heels of fire are yielding to spruce and balsam fir, characteristic species of older boreal forests on Lake Superior's north shore. The forests on the western half of Isle Royale, growing on a thick mantle of glacial till, were less disturbed by mineral exploration. Here, sugar maple and yellow birch predominate in the warmer climate of the interior hills away from Lake Superior, just as they do in the mainland forests to the south, in the Upper Peninsula of Michigan. The 19th-century wounds on both Isle Royale and the mainland were quickly covered by the lush growth of new forests, and at the beginning of the

20th century, verdant forest regrowth north of Lake Superior became prime habitat for the recovering moose population.

Evidence of possible moose presence on Isle Royale dates back to a botanical expedition in 1904, during which broken trees indicative of moose browsing were reported. Able to survive the cold waters of Lake Superior in summer but easily frightened on ice in winter, surely moose initially swam to Isle Royale. At the time of World War I, the herd had reportedly grown to a few hundred.

On Isle Royale, moose discovered a haven from predators and a virgin food supply; for almost 30 years, nothing held back their increase in numbers. The "population bomb" for Isle Royale moose exploded in the 1920s, and the herd swelled to several thousand. When biologist Adolph Murie arrived on Isle Royale in 1929, he found a habitat stretched to the breaking point. Murie reported seeing up to 30 moose in a single lake in one day, and as many as 28 moose at a mineral lick at one time. He was sure that at least 1,000 moose were present on the island, but he acknowledged that the true number might be as high as 3,000. In retrospect, the higher figure is quite reasonable; in recent decades, with 1,500 moose present, peak moose observations include "only" 17 moose in a lake in one day, and up to nine at once at a mineral lick.

After completing his field studies of moose in 1930, Murie predicted catastrophe for the Isle Royale moose population. True to his prophecy, hundreds of moose perished during severe winters in the mid-1930s. Forty dead moose were discovered in field surveys conducted in the spring of 1934. From all accounts, balsam fir, the main winter food for these moose, was in desperate condition. By 1935 Paul Hickie, a state biologist, guessed that the moose population had dropped to just 400 to 500 starving animals.

Unfortunately, there were not even any "guesstimates" made of the island's wildlife populations in the decade following the moose crash of the 1930s. Science fell between the cracks when the island was shifted from private and state hands to federal jurisdiction as a national park. During the late 1930s, the science program of the National Park Service all but evaporated, and the state of Michigan opted to confine its limited scientific efforts to the mainland. Later, World War II intervened. It was especially regrettable that little was learned about the effect of a wildfire in

1936, which burned 20 percent of the island and influenced moose habitat for decades.

In 1945, when U.S. Fish and Wildlife Service biologist Laurits Krefting flew a winter survey of Isle Royale moose in a biplane, almost all the moose he recorded were sighted in the 1936 burn area. After long flights from the Minnesota mainland (the wheel-equipped aircraft permitted no landings on the deep snow covering frozen lakes), eight transects were flown along the axis of the island. Krefting observed over 50 moose, and estimated the total population at 510 animals. Moose recovery may have been underway. Three years later, Krefting reported 12 dead moose in a spring survey and announced another major die off, fueling the belief that a "boom and bust" pattern would continue.

In 1948, a few wolf tracks were reported on Isle Royale following a cold winter with intact ice bridges to the mainland, but an abundant coyote population kept skeptics uncertain. When Ranger Bob Hakala made a plaster cast of a huge wolf track in October of 1951, wolf presence on the island was finally confirmed.

Meanwhile, Detroit newspaperman and wolf advocate Lee Smits obtained permission from the Park Service to stock the island with wolves. When a bid to obtain wild wolves failed (they were already becoming rare in Michigan's Upper Peninsula), four human-raised wolves from the Detroit Zoo were released on Isle Royale in 1952. Even though wild wolves were known to be present, the political momentum behind the introduction carried it forward. The zoo wolves, which were accustomed to relying on people, quickly became frightening pests that approached visitors looking for food, and the Park Service agreed to remove them. One was live-captured, but two others had to be shot. The fourth, "Big Jim," was not seen again.

Now that wild wolves had established themselves on Isle Royale, the stage was set for a wildlife drama never before witnessed by scientists. In 1956, NPS biologist James F. Cole recommended that the wolf-moose story become the full-time assignment of a research biologist—someone who could devote an entire career to the task. Within Cole's own agency, the advice was ignored. However, the opportunity was not lost on Durward Allen, a renowned wildlife biologist in the employ of the U.S. Fish and Wildlife Service. He had tried for several years to generate federal

As a scavenger of wolf-killed moose, the Isle Royale red fox is both a frequent beneficiary and an occasional target of wolf attack.

support within his agency for an Isle Royale study, but he gave up hope after the 1952 election swept the conservative Eisenhower administration into office. It was several more years before Allen, operating from a base at Purdue University, launched a farsighted, ongoing study of the island's wolves and moose. This was no less audacious at that time than it would be today; people are ever-impatient for quick-fix answers, and research projects generally last about as long as a graduate student's tour of duty— say three to four years.

The first wolf pack from Isle Royale to catch the world's attention was pictured in a 1963 *National Geographic* article by Durward Allen and Dave Mech. Hanging out the open window of a two-seat research aircraft with a used Argus C-3 camera, Mech captured on film for the first time spectacular scenes of a large wolf pack hunting moose. When he first saw this pack in February of 1959, Mech counted 15 wolves plus a single follower, and this group was aptly called the Big Pack. The group seemed

Antlers of moose, grown by males and
shed each year, are among the fastest-
growing tissues known.

The snowshoe hare is the "professional prey" of foxes
and birds of prey at Isle Royale. It leads a furtive
existence in protective shrubs and trees.

to claim the entire island, although a small pack of two or three wolves was often found on the finger-like projections of land at the northeast end of the island.

The Big Pack of 1959 represented the first generation or two of Isle Royale wolves—quite possibly the founders and their offspring. The Big Pack had been years in the making, and it continued to build strength and dominate the island through 1964, when researchers first glimpsed an incredible 22 wolves in this pack. However, the decline of the pack was imminent and abrupt—linked to the death of the alpha male, apparently killed by pack members in the same year.

In the late 1960s several smaller packs replaced the Big Pack, and changes were associated with the appearance of black wolves in 1967— apparently immigrants from the mainland. Their arrival spawned several episodes of violence and disruption. When the dust had settled by 1968, one black male had become established in a group of resident grays, which became the dominant West Pack.

*   *   *

In 1958, when the wolf-moose study began on Isle Royale, I was nine years old and barely aware of the world around me. I recall that *Sputnik* had been launched one year earlier, and that Dwight Eisenhower was President of the United States. However, I was more interested in Mickey Mantle, then a rising star for the Yankees, and in the Ford Edsel, an automobile that had been unveiled to dubious reviewers. These, not the doings of wolves, were the mental markers of my youthful world.

When I was a teen, I cut out and saved from the Minneapolis *Star-Tribune* some wonderful fox photos taken by Dave Mech on Isle Royale. These clippings and issues of *National Geographic* were my introduction to the island. Two hiking trips on Isle Royale while I was in college kindled a strong interest in this wild place, and I learned that Durward Allen's exciting research was based at Purdue University. While a senior in college, I wrote to Purdue and inquired about the possibility of doing graduate work with Dr. Allen, but the thick packet of material I received didn't mention wolves, moose, or Durward Allen, so I concluded that the study must have ended. It had been labeled a ten-year study in *National*

Geographic, and the decade of study ended in 1968.

Then, in November of 1969, a television documentary entitled *Wolfmen* aired, and as I watched the credits, I realized I had written to the wrong department at Purdue. I dashed off another letter and received an immediate response from Dr. Allen, requesting more information about my background and interests. Allen decided I was "the right person, in the right place, at the right time," and he offered me the next time slot for graduate work at Isle Royale. He claims he had never intended to conclude the study after ten years. He planned to continue for as long as he could obtain funding.

When finally presented with the opportunity to study wolves on Isle Royale, there was not a moment of indecision; I felt exceedingly lucky to receive such an honor. But when I arrived on the island the following summer, a skeptical chief ranger more than twice my age pointed out that we were then in the twelfth year of a "ten-year study." Occasionally I wondered, as he did, just what was left to be discovered.

A fledgling graduate student, I followed a succession of earlier researchers who had worked with Allen on the study. After Dave Mech's pioneering study of the wolves and moose, Philip Shelton had focused on beaver; Peter Jordan and Michael Wolfe had concentrated on moose population dynamics; and Wendel Johnson had studied the red fox and its mammalian prey. In the early 1970s, Durward Allen thought it best to return for another close look at the dominant predator-prey system. He had seen unprecedented events in recent winters, including very deep snow, wolves killing moose at a high rate, and even wolves running moose off cliffs. His sound intuition and long experience told him that there was still more to learn.

When I started field work on the island in 1970, the dominant pack was still the West Pack, with a black male second in command among the males. This beta male bided his time as a subordinate until he rose to the position of alpha male in 1972, when the previous pack leader disappeared. That year the new alpha male courted—and seemed to be accepted by—a small gray wolf that had been the alpha female for many years. The alpha pair was observed together twice in the summer of 1972, but then both wolves vanished. No black wolf pups were ever seen on the island, so evidently no new wolf genes from the mainland were left as a legacy.

Characteristic trees of the boreal forest—spruce, fir, aspen, and birch—dominate the northeast end of Isle Royale, close to the cooling influence of Lake Superior.

A century after disturbance by copper mining, colorful sugar maple is overtaking pioneering aspen.

Gray wolves brought themselves to Isle Royale in the late 1940s by crossing an ice bridge in winter from mainland Ontario.

A pack containing black wolves apparently invaded Isle Royale in 1967. One black wolf survived to become an alpha male by 1972. Here, the male tends an aging alpha female with a crooked (probably arthritic) front leg. Both died late in 1972 without producing any black offspring.

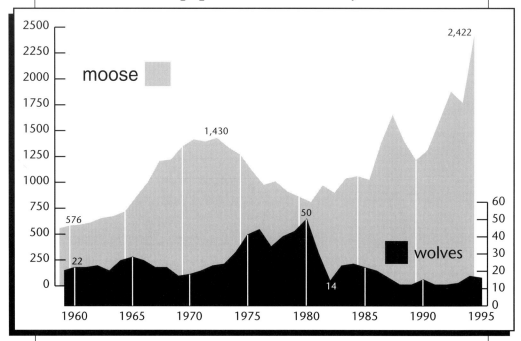

Wolf and moose populations on Isle Royale, 1959-1995

moose

2,422

1,430

576

50

22

14

wolves

1960   1965   1970   1975   1980   1985   1990   1995

The long record of wolf and moose fluctuations at Isle Royale bears no resemblance to a static balance between predator and prey. From 1959 to 1980 wolf and moose populations appeared to cycle in tandem, with wolves peaking about a decade after moose. In this period, wolves simply followed trends in their primary prey, moose over 10 years old.

All this changed in the 1980s. The crash of the wolf population in 1980-1982, initially attributed to food shortage, was later linked to a disease, canine parvovirus. High mortality of wolves in 1980-1988 reduced the population to its lowest point, but then mortality diminished as parvovirus disappeared. Wolves failed to recover, however, because some territorial packs failed to reproduce successfully. A search for the cause became a new scientific quest.

If the lack of wolf recovery has been caused by food shortage, then wolves should increase in the 1990s along with the number of old moose. After 1988 there were no diseases known to be influencing the wolf population. Genetic studies confirmed that Isle Royale wolves were inbred and had lost genetic variation because of isolation, possibly explaining poor reproduction. However, genetic decay cannot be accepted as the cause of the wolves' reproductive problems until all other explanations are eliminated. In the late 1990s alpha positions in wolf packs will be filled by a new generation of young wolves, disease-free and well-fed through their lives. Their reproductive success should shed light on the important issue of genetic variability in small, isolated populations.

A trend began in 1969 that would continue for over a decade. During that time, the wolf population increased on Isle Royale in every successive year but one—an astonishing buildup that was linked to a growing accumulation of old moose, the wolves' main prey. During those years the island was shared by three large wolf packs—the West, the Middle, and the East—and two additional packs appeared briefly in 1980, when the number of wolves reached 50.

Between 1980 and 1982, the bottom fell out of the wolf increase. Despite successful annual reproduction, there were at least 52 wolf deaths in two years. This catastrophic mortality can best be understood in the context of a new disease of the day—canine parvovirus (CPV). CPV is an acute viral disease that causes severe diarrhea and dehydration in afflicted animals, often followed by death within a couple of days. After the population made a heroic recovery in 1983, increasing from 14 wolves back up to 23, it suffered from chronic high mortality for another five years, reducing the number of wolves to just 12 by 1988. That year, the high mortality diminished just as suddenly as it had arrived years before, coincident with the disappearance of parvovirus.

Reproductive success for breeding packs on Isle Royale began to decline slowly after 1985; only one of the three territorial packs produced any living offspring between 1988 and 1993. Through the early 1990s wolves remained in the demographic doldrums, dangerously close to extinction.

In 1993 the aging alpha females in two adjacent packs shook free from whatever was ailing them, and each produced four surviving pups. Both females were dead within a year, but a new generation had finally been launched, securing for a time a tenuous future for the wolves of Isle Royale. We now watch and wait, impatiently, for the future to be revealed.

Today, as we near the end of the 20th century with almost four decades of accumulated population data, the annual monitoring of Isle Royale's wolves continues. In a world dominated and transformed by humans, Isle Royale and its wolves stand apart. As a scientist bent on probing nature's secrets, I have come to realize that in this wild enclave, which is imbedded in an often wilder Lake Superior, it is the wolves that have transformed the balance of nature, both in fact and in myth.

*A brimful beaver pond retards the runoff
of melted snow in spring and provides
habitat for a myriad of species.*

The Island Awakens

*The [national] parks are certainly too small for such a far-
ranging species as the wolf. Many animal species, for
reasons unknown, do not seem to thrive as detached
islands of populations.*
> Aldo Leopold, *A Sand County Almanac,* 1949

IN SNOW COUNTRY, IT MUST BE THE LONG PERIOD OF
anticipation, awaiting the emergence and rebirth of life,
that makes spring so extraordinary. Nowhere do I look
forward to spring as much as at Isle Royale. For several
years in the early 1970s, my wife Carolyn (Candy) and
I garnered two spaces on the first boat of the year to
Isle Royale from National Park Service headquarters in
Houghton, Michigan—a privilege we deeply
appreciated.

Perhaps it is best to go to Isle Royale by boat, as a
slow approach provides an opportunity to savor the
separation from "civilization." To cross Lake Superior
in a boat, even amidst flat calm, is to feel vulnerable.
With the mainland disappearing out the stern and
loons migrating right to left across our bow, we were
reminded of our proper place in nature—that of fellow
voyagers with other creatures. The big lake and the
remote island up ahead gradually became the "real
world."

When we reached land, we launched a 14-foot
skiff and outboard motor as quickly as possible, leaving
behind us the bustle of opening activity at park

headquarters on Mott Island. Migrating waterfowl—especially the divers that probe the deep harbors, such as buffleheads, goldeneyes, and mergansers—scattered as we motored to the edge of the ice, which still blocked access to our summer field headquarters, an old commercial fishing camp on Rock Harbor called Bangsund Cabin. The Park Service assumed responsibility for this dwelling after fisherman Jack Bangsund died there in his sleep in October of 1959. Since that time (indeed, for more years than the commercial fishing operation lasted at the site), it has served as a cherished research base.

In midsummer, there is occasionally time for attention to the deteriorating foundation—logs simply laid atop the rocks of the beach. But in spring, there is no time to lose on such ancillary matters. We shoved the mountain of gear across the ice to the gravel beach, opened the musty cabin to the fresh spring air, and quickly stashed boxes and bags of gear inside in order to take an early look at the island in the evening.

It was a great delight to be the first humans walking on an Isle Royale trail in late April. The trails had accumulated sign (animal tracks, wolf scat, shed antlers of bull moose, and, rarely, a chewed moose bone) for six months, and they now carried the residue of numerous dramas. However, we could only guess at what had really occurred. Where our eyes detected scattered clauses, a wolf's nose would read whole chapters.

In our first spring we were puzzled by the lack of wolf tracks on the Daisy Farm Trail, which runs along the northeast end of the island near our Rock Harbor research cabin. When we topped the Greenstone Ridge and climbed Ojibway Fire Tower, however, we found that all the interior lakes were ice-covered, and realized that wolves were still using their preferred highways.

Surprises seem synonymous with spring. In our first trek along the Greenstone Ridge in 1975, our overly optimistic plan to reach Hatchet Lake in the island's midsection was cut short by aching muscles and sunset. At 10:30 p.m., we quickly pitched our tent in the last hint of daylight and fired up the Optimus stove we used for cooking. In those days, we were enjoying our first lightweight backpacking tents, having just retired a venerable and memorable old canvas tent from Abercrombie and Fitch—one of Durward Allen's early investments in field gear. The new-fangled nylon tent didn't require the cutting of tent poles, but it did require a taut line tied to a stake at front and back, to prevent a swayback that would catch water. When a winter wren awakened us with its enthusiastic song at 5 a.m. the next morning, we were dismayed to find the tent collapsed around us.

"It must be my spouse's fault," we both thought, and I unzipped the front flap so I could step out and remedy the situation. We had a good laugh as we beheld the scene outside. Our world was blanketed with several inches of heavy, wet snow that had fallen silently all night. The only sensible thing to do was to go back to sleep, hoping for warm spring sunshine.

Just days after this cold interlude, we were baking in the bright sun of the open ridge and looking forward to the deep shade of the mature maple-birch forest at the island's west end. The realities of early spring again elicited a chuckle as we reached these old forests and belatedly remembered that trees without leaves provide no shade! Early-blooming flowers like hepatica and spring beauty take advantage of this seasonal window in the canopy, completing the important business of growth and reproduction before the light is intercepted by emerging leaves.

We give the wolves a wide berth at this time of year—there is time in summer to count pups by listening to their howling, and disturbing the dens in spring might harm the pups. When newborn pups appear, usually during the third week of April (63 days after mating, usually in the third week of February), wolf packs suddenly shift from a nomadic existence to inhabiting a solid base at traditional den sites.

Only once have we probed the wolves' affairs in spring—in 1976, when we had only a few days to determine whether the East Pack had reproduced in its traditional den. Candy and I briefly entered their domain, quietly walking down wolf trails that had become familiar to us over the previous three years. As we neared the suspected den, where pups had been born the year before, it became obvious that there was new activity. Wolf tracks covered each muddy depression, and fresh scat was increasingly evident. This pack had included 16 members the previous winter, and traffic in the vicinity of the den was heavy. The air was completely still, and we took the chance that the wolves would not detect us. We stole toward the den site, an abandoned beaver lodge now situated in a dry and grassy meadow. As the lodge came into view, we left the wolf trail and hid behind a tangle of dead trees, waiting for some sign of occupancy.

Bangsund cabin on Rock Harbor, once the home of a commercial fisherman, has housed wolf researchers since the late 1950s.

An unmistakable sign of spring, the appearance of hepatica precedes the emergence of shade-producing leaves on trees in the deciduous forest at Isle Royale.

In the courtship arena, or lek, a male sharp-tailed grouse displays yellow "eyebrows" and inflated throat sacs to gain the attention of females. This species declined as forests matured and evidently disappeared from Isle Royale in the late 1980s.

Abruptly, a wolf arrived from a different direction and appeared in the beaver meadow. Making its way straight for the lodge, it stopped on top of the mound and greeted a wolf that had just emerged from a "doorway." With eyes and gestures, Candy and I communicated our excitement and prepared to leave. The pack had reproduced, and that was all we needed to know. As we tiptoed away, we heard another wolf approaching on "our" path. Again we quietly left the path and crouched behind some shrubs, our hearts beating almost audibly. Amazingly, the wolf walked right by us, simply intent on getting home.

*   *   *

We placed a premium on extensive travel in the spring, and while wolves and moose were our primary focus, we were interested in all the players on the island, for one species should not be studied in isolation from its neighbors. In the early 1970s, we discovered the island's last known courtship arena for sharp-tailed grouse. The most powerful flyer among grouse species that live in the Great Lakes region, the sharptail was the only grouse species known to inhabit Isle Royale. It attracted little attention until it disappeared; then Chris Martin assembled a chronicle that described much of the forest history of the island.

In the 1920s grouse were regularly flushed from the trails near Rock Harbor Lodge, and they were recorded in considerable numbers across the island. One observer tallied some 80 birds during a six-mile hike from the lodge to Mt. Franklin. At that time young stands of birch and aspen predominated in the forests across the eastern end of the island, with extensive patches of shrub growth that succeeded the burns dating from copper exploration in the latter half of the 19th century. Birds usually have invariant preferences for specific habitat types, and the low shrubs and frequent openings of the regenerating forest on Isle Royale that were prevalent early in this century perfectly suited the needs of sharptails. The sharptail's preference for open country actually explains its presence on Isle Royale; even if it was unable to fly the entire distance from the mainland at once, this bird would be comfortable landing on open ice for a few rest stops.

Good sharptail grouse habitat is of short duration in forested areas where natural fires are rare, as on an island in the middle of Lake Superior. In the 1970s balsam fir and white spruce succeeded deciduous trees and shrubs on the eastern half of Isle Royale, and openings disappeared. When the island's first superintendent, George Baggley, returned in 1989 after an absence of more than 50 years, he was astonished and disappointed by the remarkable transformation. The vibrant, thick stands of paper birch and aspen that had lined the shores of Rock Harbor in the 1930s were falling down everywhere, and a thick growth of spruce and fir obscured the lower layer of the forest.

The sharp-tailed grouse tracked the pattern of forest regrowth in textbook fashion. The birds were seen everywhere in the 1920s, but fewer and fewer sightings were reported in each decade thereafter. In 1962, along the top of Feldtman Ridge, beaver researcher Philip Shelton recorded seeing them for the last time on the western half of Isle Royale, where older forests are more prevalent. In 1970, field assistant John Vanada and I happened onto a brood of young grouse on the top of Greenstone Ridge near Mt. Siskiwit, an area that had been burned over in 1936. Three years later, I saw grouse on this ridge for the last time.

In early May of 1973, Candy and I slept overnight in Ojibway Tower, trying to get a jump on the next day's trek down the island. At 5 a.m., I was awakened by an odd hooting, like that of a pigeon. There were no pigeons on the island, so I climbed out of my warm sleeping bag and clumsily found my way out onto the tower's walkway, 60 feet above the ground. Looking through the grate that formed the walkway floor, I saw a grouse perched on the tower supports and two dancing males that faced each other in a serious display of virility in the middle of the park trail.

The ridgetop on Mt. Ojibway is covered with juneberry, chokecherry, and hazelnut. Moose relentlessly browse these woody shrubs back to a central stem or to snow-level each winter, inadvertently maintaining a suitable area where birds gather to dance their courtship rituals. I had never seen the spectacle myself, and I couldn't pass up the opportunity to try to photograph it. I tiptoed down the many flights of steel stairs to ground level, but I needn't have been so careful, because the birds were totally focused on each other in the low light of pre-dawn.

One female stood at the edge of the arena, calmly watching the dancing males or browsing the chopped-off cherry plants nearby. The males, meanwhile, were alternately frozen in mid-step with head low, purple throat sacs distended, and wings outstretched, or were beating the ground in a frenzied dance while twirling around the center of the clearing, a dancing grounds known as a grouse lek. Their bright yellow brows were also distended and seemed to be a target for pecking during brief skirmishes. Occasionally, a grouse would draw blood with a quick stab of the beak. During such contests, one male vanquished the others and filed off with the watchful female, with whom he presumably mated.

To my knowledge, this was the only grouse lek ever described on Isle Royale, and it was certainly the last. Only three males and one female were seen on Mt. Ojibway in 1976 in our last springtime visit. Ten years later, we searched in vain for the characteristic orange winter droppings of grouse along the ridgetop. In 1986 Robert Nobles, a volunteer in the park, flushed a single grouse at Mt. Ojibway in early May, and Chris Martin saw a single male on a nearby ridgetop that seemed to be courting without benefit of a female audience. No grouse have been seen since. They became extinct because Isle Royale's forests had steadily recovered from human-caused disturbance a century earlier.

Bone marrow, the last store of fat in a moose, turns gelatinous before a moose dies of malnutrition.

As the green leaves of hazelnut emerge in spring, this thin moose will be able to rebuild the body mass that was lost in order to survive winter.

Moose with serious injuries such as this broken leg are rapidly culled by attentive wolves at Isle Royale.

In response to irritation caused by winter ticks, moose may
rub off much of their hair in late winter, aggravating
their precarious physical status in spring.

Down on its "wrists," a cow moose in July sucks
the spring dry to supplement the meager sodium
supply provided by terrestrial plants.

It is a common experience for us to see more dead moose than live moose during our early spring travels on Isle Royale. Collecting bone specimens from dead moose had been a regular activity throughout all previous years of study, and I continued the tradition enthusiastically. In 1970, our autopsy file contained sex and age information on over 500 Isle Royale moose recovered since 1958. Most of these dead moose were wolf kills spotted in winter from aircraft, but field work by geologist King Huber from 1967 to 1969 suggested that more could be done. While bushwacking through the interior of the island, off the park trails, Huber often found moose bones. His reports led the wolf-moose team to 44 moose skeletons in the summer of 1969. In my first summer of field work, while I was learning the island mostly from its trails, we recovered only 12 kills.

My first spring field season came the next year, when we found out how much easier it is to see bones in May, before "green-up." In 1971 I recruited another eager graduate student, James Dietz, to help in this effort. Candy, my wife of less than a year, wished us well as she dropped us off on the Moskey Basin dock for our first expedition. We had a week's worth of food and a reservation on the boat *Voyageur* for the return trip from the other end of the island. Jim and I planned to hike 12 miles cross-country to Malone Bay, then another eight miles to Hay Bay on the second day. Within a few hours, we realized our plans were overly ambitious.

The winter of 1970-71 had been the third deep-snow winter in a row, and moose were dying from malnutrition as well as from wolves. Whereas census figures had shown about 1,300 moose on the island in 1969, winter and wolves were now obviously taking their toll. Jim and I found eight dead moose during our first day out, and we were soon bogged down with a heavy load of bones.

More troubles awaited us at the west end of Isle Royale, where a vast lowland called Siskiwit Swamp covers some 20 square miles. We were amateur navigators, aided by the standard topographical map and some black-and-white aerial photos taken in 1957, and the island was unforgiving. There were avenues through the swamp, old beachlines of Lake Superior dating from earlier times when the lake level was higher. If we could find these beachlines and stay on them, we could make good progress and keep our feet dry.

After probing the center of the swamp successfully, Jim and I straddled a fallen cedar and enjoyed a congratulatory lunch of peanut butter and crackers. We calculated that we were adjacent to the narrowest part of the swamp; if we just plowed through the adjacent alders for a few hundred yards, we would come to the Big Siskiwit River, where we could hope to cross at a beaver dam and then scamper to dry land and a park trail.

Unfortunately, we had taken the wrong fork of a narrow beachline. As we set off for the other side of the swamp, we were actually heading for its wettest part, almost a mile wide. The alders gave way to wet grass, which gradually became more open water than grass. Still thinking we were just a few yards from our goal, Jim and I pushed ahead, jumping from hummock to hummock and tossing cameras back and forth to whomever was on firmest footing. The swamp crossing, which should have taken half an hour, consumed the afternoon.

This initial trip, although difficult, convinced us that a wealth of information lay on the forest floor at Isle Royale. The following year we hired two assistants who formed one team, and Candy and I hiked as a second team. One overnight expedition yielded specimens from a dozen dead moose. We once found a carcass with five legs; a little extra searching produced the parts we needed to complete a second autopsy report. A cow and calf moose had both been killed by wolves.

Dead moose were easy to find once we left park trails in the spring, but live moose seemed to be in hiding in May. We eventually found that they favored certain locales. These sites, called moose licks, have a barnyard smell and are the focus of a network of trails beaten into the earth by generations of moose in an annual trek to replenish their sodium reserves. At Isle Royale most sodium licks are located at the southwest end of the island, where they are associated with glacial features called drumlins—lines of glacial till laid down as glaciers retreated from west to east across Isle Royale.

About 8,000 years ago, most of the land that now forms Isle Royale lay beneath a retreating mass of continental ice. The glaciers stalled midway down the island, so the western portion of the island was probably freed from the grip of the glaciers hundreds of years before the east end. The glacier strewed tons of till across the new landscape, burying bedrock under a layer tens of yards deep. The remainder of the island was scraped when glacial retreat accelerated, leaving deep gouges in the exposed basalt

Physiologist Ulysses Seal studies his former quarry at a spring in May. The moose was radiocollared as it replenished its supply of sodium, a vital element in the moose diet.

Ticks, still looking for a suitable host animal to help them complete their life cycle, climb to the highest part of a moose after it dies. Then they simply wait for another moose to pass by.

bedrock. The result, which has ramifications today for the island's wild inhabitants, was a pattern of deep till and thick soils on the west end of Isle Royale, while the east end consists of primal bedrock covered by a thin layer of organic material that took thousands of years to accumulate.

Deep in the glacial till at the west end of Isle Royale are a few patches of sodium-rich minerals, and the leachate from some of these sites has slowly been funneled by impervious layers within drumlins and glacial moraines to final release at the surface through tiny springs.

Sodium-starved in spring, Isle Royale moose are attracted to these small, mineral-rich rivulets. By following moose trails, we have located about two dozen such licks.

In the course of drinking them dry and patiently waiting for a refill, a moose may spend several days in the vicinity of a lick, tanking up on sodium. Research by Peter Jordan and Gary Belovsky revealed that terrestrial vegetation on Isle Royale contains too little sodium to sustain moose. For unknown reasons, aquatic plants concentrate sodium. Before mid-June, however, when plants begin to emerge on pond bottoms, a few mineral licks provide the only important source of the vital element. Moose hooves have carved deep ruts in the earth along traditional paths to these licks, where for decades the huge herbivores have secured a scarce commodity.

In 1929, biologist Adolph Murie frequented moose licks when he began the first scientific study of Isle Royale moose. For two summers Murie camped at Lake Eva, in the island's interior, where he observed a parade of moose—often a dozen or more at a time. Such gatherings of moose are memorable. The air was electric with nervous tension on one occasion when I saw nine moose, all bulls, standing within a 50-foot circle at watchful attention over a lick, each primed to bolt at the slightest provocation.

Forty-five years after Murie's study, I sought the same moose haunts that Murie had described, but I was surprised and disappointed to find them all gone. None of the mineral licks Murie used in his study could be located in the 1970s. The Lake Eva lick, in particular, had been the site of a blind erected for guests at the Belle Isle Resort, located a few miles down the harbor. Fisherman Milford Johnson was hired to transport lodge guests by boat to a landing near Lake Eva, and although I found the spike in a shoreline tree where Milford had tied his boat, the lick had vanished.

Perhaps the sodium source buried in the glacial till had finally been exhausted.

Despite the boost given to moose by sodium-rich licks in spring, the survivors of winter's rigors are often on the edge of death from malnutrition, and a delay of a week or two in the green-up of vegetation may push them over the line. Moose on Isle Royale present a ragtag appearance at winter's end, all because of a tiny ectoparasite known as the winter tick.

Winter ticks, or moose ticks, climb onto moose as pinhead-sized larvae in October. Through a succession of blood meals taken from their hosts, the ticks grow to adult size by midwinter, still constituting only a minor annoyance. In their last blood meal, taken only by females for egg-laying purposes, the ticks balloon up to a half-inch in diameter, and the moose vigorously rub against trees and even bite off their own hair because of the irritation. Bare patches of skin may be seen in January, and by early March moose may suffer from major hair loss.

An enormous number of ticks can climb onto an individual moose. University of Alberta biologist William Samuels has spent years studying the effects of ticks on moose. By dividing up the hide of a moose into sectors and doing several representative counts, he has estimated the number of ticks on individual moose. Bill agreed to look at the hides of two Isle Royale moose that perished in the winter of 1989. Severely weakened by blood loss and malnutrition induced by ticks, an adult cow had fallen down a shoreline embankment and dislocated her shoulder, never to rise again. She harbored an estimated 25,000 ticks! A malnourished calf that died in February had hosted 30,000 ticks. Unperturbed, Bill commented that these were actually rather light infestations for moose that die of tick-related causes. In Alberta, he has recorded up to 100,000 ticks on a single animal.

For an adult moose with a huge body mass of heat-producing muscle, hair loss to ticks may not be a serious problem. However, researcher Ed Addison of the Ontario Ministry of Natural Resources studied captive calf moose that had lost hair to ticks. The calves shivered almost constantly during the inevitable cold rains of April. Hypothermia, added to anemia from blood loss and toxins injected by ticks, can clearly affect the viability of moose on Isle Royale.

*   *   *

In May of 1984, we needed to radiocollar a few moose at Isle Royale for a study of feeding behavior being conducted by graduate student Ken Risenhoover. Mineral licks provided the sites we needed to immobilize moose for the radiocollaring procedures, using drugs delivered by dart gun. In late May many moose could be seen at close range around a mineral lick within a short period of time. Incredibly, we collared 20 moose in just a few days at a single lick, and we passed up many more in order to get an equal number of females and males. Capture specialists Steven Schmitt from Michigan and Ulysses (Ulie) Seal from Minnesota assisted, anxious to try a powerful new immobilizing drug—a narcotic called carfentanil. Here we learned that Isle Royale moose were in poor shape in spring, requiring reduced doses of the drug. Carfentanil immobilizes moose, but it also has other physiological effects. Experiments performed on other species have shown it to be an anesthetic and an addictive painkiller.

On the first day we successfully collared a couple of bull moose, decreasing the dose to provide a safe experience for all concerned. Even so, immobilization in spring produced considerable short-term stress for the moose, and they were quite anxious to vacate the capture area as soon as they regained their feet. However, on the second day of the operation, the first moose to appear was an animal we had collared the day before, an old bull that suffered from many of life's accumulated ills. This bull simply stood in the mineral lick, broadside and at close range to Ulie Seal, who sat waiting with a loaded dart gun. Ulie speculated that we had perhaps given the old bull moose a few pain-free hours, and now he wanted more!

Many of the 20 moose we collared survived for four or five years, and their radio signals provided useful information on habitat use, activity patterns, feeding preferences, and survival and reproduction rates. Collared moose were also used to analyze aerial census efficiency. This was the first time any wildlife species had been radiocollared at Isle Royale, and the Park Service was concerned about disrupting visitor opportunities for viewing and photographing animals. So we carefully camouflaged the collars and chose a site as far away as possible from park trails and campgrounds. But many of the collared moose arrived back in the Windigo visitor area before we had completed the operation. I asked the rangers to keep track of any comments they received on the collared moose. To my knowledge, the only advice the Park Service received was from a visitor who suggested that each moose should be visibly numbered, so hikers could tell one from another!

*   *   *

Oddly, it was during the moose collaring operation that I first faced the issue of loss of genetic variability in Isle Royale wolves. Ulie Seal was already caught up in the rapidly developing field of conservation biology, and as he sat against a birch tree in the middle of Siskiwit Swamp, waiting with his dart gun for a cooperative moose, he began to ponder the issue of inbreeding among Isle Royale wolves. Not only are the small number of wolves and their isolation potential problems, Ulie argued, but so is the *effective* population size, which is roughly approximated by the number of breeding individuals. On Isle Royale, the effective population is almost laughably small—usually four to six wolves. Such a population, Ulie mused, would lose about 15 percent of its genetic variability with each generation.

In captive populations of many species of wildlife, such genetic decay often leads to poor reproduction, called inbreeding depression. The absence of genetic problems in Isle Royale wolves up to that time might be attributed to the exceptionally long life spans of breeding alpha wolves, which were safe from traps, guns, and other instruments of death. A similar strategy is sometimes used in captive breeding programs for endangered species, one of Ulie's specialties, when reproduction is associated with increased risk of mortality. By extending the life span of breeders and delaying reproduction as long as possible, each generation is drawn out to its maximum.

Even as Ulie raised these points, Isle Royale wolves were entering a period of continuous high attrition. Their annual mortality rate of 30 to 40 percent, prevalent through the 1980s, was comparable to what mainland populations faced in areas where hunting and trapping were substantial. We knew little about the nature of this mortality, except that it killed animals after we saw them as nine-month-old pups. Here Ulie raised another warning flag, in the form of the new disease, canine parvovirus (CPV). Caused by a mutant virus first recognized in 1977, CPV was highly lethal in domestic dog populations around the world, causing death from acute diarrhea and dehydration in up to half of the young dogs exposed to the virus. In 1983 CPV killed 11 of 12 wolf pups and yearlings in a captive wolf pack maintained by Seal and Dave Mech near Minneapolis. Only then did wolf researchers begin to consider seriously what this disease might mean to wild wolf populations.

There were certainly compelling hints that CPV might have already become important at Isle Royale. The disease spread around the earth within a few months after it was initially discovered. A new mutant variety appeared in 1980, and its quick, worldwide dispersal was, according to many veterinarians, associated with a new outbreak among dogs.

In 1981 the deadly dog virus reached Houghton, Michigan, my home-town and a point of departure for many visitors to Isle Royale. Sick and dying dogs were brought by the score to the three local veterinarians, and dog owners were reminded that a new vaccine was available to protect their pets.

The local appearance of parvovirus coincided with a spectacular crash in the Isle Royale wolf population, including the unprecedented loss of all nine pups born in 1981—distributed in three packs. But disease was not yet a part of the scientific paradigm of population regulation and, without positive evidence, it was easy to table the disease issue. We did search for clues by testing wolf scat for antibodies, by blood-sampling red foxes for disease screening, and even by searching through the contents of wolf scat with an electron microscope—all to no avail. This is where we left the problem for four more years.

By 1988, it was clear that wolf extinction might be imminent, as mortality remained high and the number of new pups declined each year. The prospect of immediate wolf extinction jolted park managers and scientists out of the prevailing conservative attitude about handling the wolves themselves. The isolated wolf population might be experiencing genetic problems, or it could be suffering from introduced disease. Or the wolves might simply be facing a periodic food shortage, as had been expected in the late 1980s because few moose calves had survived in the late 1970s. Without handling the wolves, we would never learn whether their problems were caused by genetics, disease, lack of food, or something else entirely.

Live-trapping of the Isle Royale wolves began in the spring of 1988. For almost ten years, I had accumulated wolf traps and parts of traps in

Yearling female #1071 was immobilized and radiocollared in 1994, then checked for disease exposure and sampled for genetic characteristics before she was released. Assisting were David Soleim and veterinarian Mark Johnson (right) of the National Park Service.

In the 1970s, an alpha female wolf of long standing produced an unusually large number of offspring that were noteworthy for their "rope-tails" (top), probably a manifestation of unique genetic characteristics within the small Isle Royale population.

Female wolf #600, pictured with the author, became a social outcast of her own pack after losing her pups and her alpha position to her sister, female #450, in 1989. She trailed the pack until her death a year and a half later.

Male wolf #420 was a large and healthy wolf, but he reproduced poorly as an alpha male in the West Pack from 1987 to 1993. During this time, while controlling half of Isle Royale, the West Pack declined from eight wolves to just an alpha pair.

my basement, should they ever be needed. Such equipment had been retired long ago by commercial suppliers, so wolf traps were antique commodities relegated to collectors' shelves.

The steel traps we employed were little changed from the original 1840s design by Sewell Newhouse of Oneida, New York. Such traps, combined with firearms and, after 1875, strychnine, had made short work of eliminating the wolf from the United States. Later, a few trap modifications made it possible to hold a live wolf safely, and the trap became an important wolf research tool for Dave Mech in Minnesota. Wolves are usually caught at night, and traps are checked each morning. If all goes well, each wolf is detained for just a short time for processing.

For a long time I had been of two minds about capturing wolves on Isle Royale. I understood and completely agreed with the scientific necessity for the work, realizing that it would benefit the wolves in the long run. Yet I could not easily accept the notion that generations of wolf freedom on Isle Royale would be compromised by human dictates, however brief and well-intentioned. Isle Royale wolves had never lost their fear of people, and their vestigial antipathy toward humans would soon be refreshed. I could only hope that everything would go smoothly, and at the same time develop a contingency plan for every conceivable thing that might go wrong. If mistakes were made, they had better be made by me.

In May of 1988, after maintaining traps on just a few miles of hiking trails, four wolves (one-third of the remaining population) had been caught without incident. The animals were blood-sampled for disease and genetic studies, then released with radio collars that would enable us to maintain year-round contact with each wolf.

After a close examination, some clues regarding the wolves' troubles were obvious. They were *not* starving. In fact, the wolves were much larger and heavier than I had expected, suggesting that they had enjoyed relative prosperity through their lives. Food shortage, however, might occur at other times of the year, and we could only be sure that wolves had plenty to eat in midwinter, when they were under daily surveillance. Years of poor moose calf survival in the mid-1970s meant that few old moose were around in the late 1980s. Perhaps we were only witnessing a wolf population trough a bit lower than expected based on one previous "cycle" in wolves and moose.

Food shortage, disease, or genetics—one of these might explain the wolf doldrums of the late 1980s. I hoped for, but did not expect, a quick answer. Indeed, many years were to pass, revealing several surprises, before rudimentary answers would take shape.

Two of the four wolves captured in 1988 tested positive for canine parvovirus. More difficult to understand, however, was that two of the wolves had *not* been exposed to this disease. If we had found the disease that was decimating the population, all of the wolves should have been exposed to it. A year later, two wolves tested marginally positive to parvovirus, then all evidence of the disease vanished. It seemed that parvovirus had come and gone.

Genetic studies by Robert Wayne and his colleagues at UCLA were revealing. Using mitochondrial DNA, a tiny loop of DNA outside a cell's nucleus, we expected to find the obvious link between mainland wolves in Ontario and those on Isle Royale. But the Isle Royale wolf genotype could not be found in the first several dozen mainland wolves we studied. Eventually, with almost 250 Ontario wolves tested, the ancestral genetic link matching Isle Royale wolves was found, in one wolf taken by a trapper about 50 miles north of Lake Superior. The rarity of the mainland linkage, combined with the genetic uniformity of Isle Royale wolves, indicated that there was only one founding event, a single ancestor for all generations of wolves at Isle Royale. Oddly, the mitochondrial DNA of Isle Royale wolves was derived from mainland coyotes, evidence of low-level hybridization between wolves and coyotes that predated their arrival on Isle Royale.

DNA fingerprinting showed the wolves to be highly inbred, comparable to members of a single family. Further analysis revealed that wolves on Isle Royale had lost roughly 50% of the genetic variability of mainland wolves. This was all evidence of remarkable isolation for the small population of island wolves, providing an acid test for the notion that inbred populations are not viable.

Some of the carefree nature of springtime trips to Isle Royale disappeared after 1988. As I became wrapped up in the engrossing wolf mystery at Isle Royale, live-capture efforts in early spring became an important addition to my annual schedule. No one guessed that it might take 10 years to find the answers.

*Before collecting bone specimens, the author (left) and
a team of Earthwatch volunteers inspect the intact
skeleton of a moose that died from starvation in 1992.*

Earthwatchers

Few laymen realize that every bone that one holds in one's hand is a fallen kingdom . . . a unique object that will never return through time.
  Loren Eiseley, *The Lost Notebooks of Loren Eiseley,* 1987

IN 1958, AT THE TOP OF MAUNA LOA ON THE ISLAND of Hawaii, atmospheric scientist Charles Keeling began recording the amount of carbon dioxide in the atmosphere. The same year, on the other side of the planet, Dave Mech began picking up the bones of wolf-killed moose at Isle Royale. The only link between these two efforts, at that time, was that they were the beginnings of important long-term monitoring programs. Thirty years later, the two records combined in a way that could never have been anticipated.

Bones tell many stories, and deciphering these records has become a very sophisticated process. In 1989, when the Shroud of Turin (thought to be Christ's burial cloth) was being dated using Oxford University's accelerator mass spectrometer, Jeffrey Bada stood next in line with small vials of gaseous extracts from Isle Royale moose teeth. Bada, a geochemist at Scripp's Institution of Oceanography, determined the levels of radioactive carbon in teeth from Isle Royale moose, reflecting amounts deposited during nuclear weapons testing conducted by the Cold War super-powers in the early 1960s. What started as an effort to ascribe a date of death to bones of wolves and moose that were located years after the animals had died became a revealing study of carbon and nitrogen, the elemental building blocks of all plants and animals.

Based on earlier work by Jeff Bada, we had expected to find, by using bomb radiocarbon, that moose incorporated carbon into their teeth when they were calves, at the time of tooth formation. We also expected to learn that this carbon was "locked up" thereafter, inert and encased in enamel. Indeed, this is exactly what Bada discovered when he and the moose teeth visited Oxford.

The surprises came when we looked at the long-term pattern of naturally occurring isotopes of carbon—isotopes that behave the same chemically, but differ in the number of neutrons found in their nucleus. We had a 75-year record of moose teeth to examine, with belated thanks to biologist Adolph Murie, who in 1929 and 1930 had collected skulls from a few moose that he shot or found dead on Isle Royale. Based on a hunch that the bones might someday be useful, Murie had filled three large cabinets at the University of Michigan's Museum of Zoology.

The modern-day curator of these bones, Philip Myers, generously allowed us to remove small portions of teeth from these early moose. Coupled with moose bones collected by the wolf-moose team since 1958, a chronology of moose teeth existed for most of the 20th century, and the fluctuations in carbon isotopes they revealed were a genuine eye-opener. Moose, unknowingly acting as biological time capsules, had stored in their teeth a record of large-scale ecological change. While the deciphering of this record continues today, evidence indicates that the wildfire of 1936 had a major influence on nutrient cycles on the island. In addition to mirroring such local phenomena, the carbon in moose teeth from Isle Royale revealed the same inexorable rise in carbon dioxide, due to worldwide combustion of fossil fuels, that Keeling's instruments detected at Mauna Loa.

Individually, moose occupy home ranges that cover ten percent or less of Isle Royale, so the plants (and isotopes) they consume exhibit much local variation. Each plant species—in fact, each individual plant—has a different complement of isotopes in its tissues, depending on a bewilder-ing complex of ecological processes, including photosynthesis, nitrogen fixation, water balance, and others. As a consumer of huge quantities of plants, a moose accumulates carbon and nitrogen from the vegetative communities within its home range.

Wolves, on the other hand, may range over the entire island, so their teeth record correspondingly larger-scale events. As pups, the proteins stored in their teeth contain carbon that only a few months earlier existed as CO_2 in the atmosphere. Plants pull the CO_2 out of the air, incorporating it into their leaves and new twigs through photosynthesis. Moose eat the leaves and twigs, and most moose are eventually eaten by wolves.

Amazingly, the record left behind in wolves' teeth homogenizes all the details of these ecological exchanges, retaining only the record of atmospheric change in carbon dioxide. As we humans continue to burn up the world's store of fossil fuels, we are not only increasing the CO_2 level in the atmosphere, perhaps changing global climate, but we are also changing the relative amounts of carbon-12 and carbon-13, two naturally occurring isotopes of carbon. Fossil fuels have relatively more carbon-12 than present-day atmospheric carbon, and so through modern technology we are also increasing the relative abundance of carbon-12 in the atmosphere. This isotope pattern is of no consequence except as a record of change—one that is stored in the Greenland ice sheet, in coral reefs around the world, and . . . in wolves on Isle Royale.

In the island's wilderness, which is as pristine as any in the continental United States, wolves have inadvertently recorded the two largest atmospheric perturbations generated by modern humans—the radioactive fallout from thermonuclear weapons and the accelerating rise in CO_2 from the combustion of fossil fuels. For any thinking human, this should underscore the scale of the modern human enterprise, and should hint at the magnitude of the challenge of maintaining natural processes in our national parks. There is no place on the planet that remains unaffected by human technology, and the most insidious of all environmental risks are those we cannot see.

"What will you *do* with all those bones?" is a frequent question visitors ask when they stop at our summer research cabin. My answer is usually complicated and lengthy—after all, the bones have been our most reliable clues to the mysteries of wolf-moose dynamics. But sometimes I reply, without shame, "I really don't know." Surely, researchers who follow me will glean even more information from these specimens. And in June of 1994 Gendron Jensen, an artist in residence on Isle Royale, taught me yet another use for the bone collection. Gendron's massive yet meticulous

This rare photograph of an Isle Royale wolf was taken in 1973, as the wolf visited a mineral lick frequented by moose.

The interior of a beaver lodge that was used as a whelping den by the East Pack for three consecutive years in the early 1990s.

Candy Peterson examines an abandoned beaver lodge that was a favorite whelping den for the East Pack in the 1970s. Wolves enlarged the beaver passageways for their own use.

After a wildfire in 1936 that burned one-fifth of
Isle Royale, the emerging forest of aspen was good
moose habitat for almost three decades.

The author, headnetted against mosquitoes, hoists the
skeleton of a wolf-killed moose that was spotted in
winter from an aircraft and recovered in summer.

drawings, depicting many bones I had discarded, captured a power and energy I had never appreciated. After serving in many careers, including seven years with Benedictine monks, Gendron now considers himself a full-time "bone artist." If there is soul in animal bones, he comes closer to revealing it than anyone else I know. Loren Eiseley maintained that "there is a natural history of souls, nay, even of man himself, which can be learned only from the symbolism inherent in the world about him."

*   *   *

For almost 40 years, a summer mission of our field research has been to scour the island for bones. In midsummer the understory vegetation on Isle Royale often reaches head level, obscuring one's feet and one's partner. For safety's sake, we travel in pairs when off-trail, so at least one member of a team can go for help in case of disaster.

By trial and error, mostly the latter, one comes to learn valuable rules of travel in the woods, a code that helps keep body and soul together. Condensed, the code goes something like this: carry a good compass, consult it frequently, and always trust it; realize that a new beaver dam is treacherous—once you start slipping in the mud on the upstream side, prepare to get wet; remember that dead birch logs on the ground provide soft footing but lousy support and soggy sit-upons; and, when your pack is tangled in the branches of a white cedar, don't fight it—cedar branches dangle you by a long leash before pulling you up short.

Candy and I share an insatiable appetite to explore, and we forged a tight partnership over thousands of Isle Royale miles. Her appetite is more easily satisfied than my own, however. Early in the summer, the daily 17 hours of daylight allow hiking until almost 10:30 p.m. Once, early in our marriage, we were busy in the interior of the island and I thought I'd saved just enough time to get us out to the lakeshore by 10 p.m., allowing us a comfortable amount of time in which to set up a tent and cook supper before dark. But the final three-quarter-mile trek to the shore, which I thought might take 30 minutes, instead required twice as long, as we encountered an unanticipated stretch of downed trees. When darkness overtook us, Lake Superior was nowhere in sight.

Exasperated and exhausted, Candy grew very quiet, issuing occasional

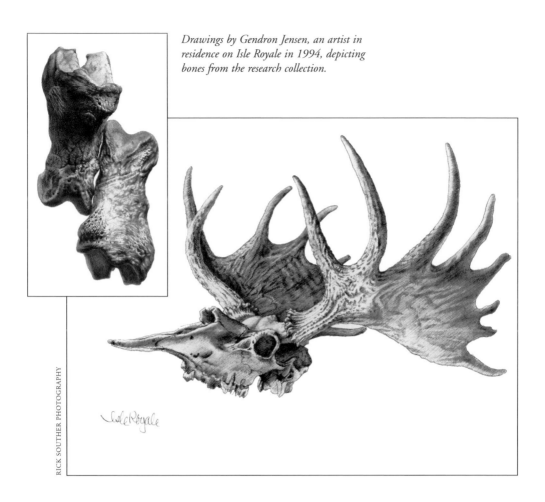

Drawings by Gendron Jensen, an artist in residence on Isle Royale in 1994, depicting bones from the research collection.

expressions of disgust. This was not a good sign. The night was moonless, overcast, and inky black as we emerged on the shoreline, and I had to find my way on hands and knees to the water's edge, in order to fill a pot with water for supper. Things will get better with a warm meal inside us, I thought, as we huddled around the red-hot stove—our only source of sound and light. After 20 minutes the stew was finally ready and, trying to redeem myself, I rose to fetch our cups and spoons. But my knee hooked the pot handle, and the pot was summarily upended, spilling its contents on the ground. We did not carry enough food for this contingency, so we headed for the tent with only a candy bar to eat. Weeks, even years, later, Candy would relate this story, together with the admission that it was the only time the prospect of divorce crossed her mind!

A beaming and freshly showered Earthwatch team poses with the annual collection of moose bones gathered by researchers.

On display but no longer functional, moose skulls with antlers have accumulated in the research collection.

Low-lying coniferous forests, used heavily by moose in winter,
contain a disproportionate number of moose skeletons. The period
of greatest mortality for moose is winter and early spring.

Few people, I think, would consider cross-country backpacking on Isle Royale an enjoyable undertaking. Vistas are infrequent; your feet (which you can rarely see) are always wet; and your shins and face are marked by all the large and small branches, logs, and twigs that get in the way. So it was with some trepidation in 1988 that we agreed to cooperate with a Boston-based organization called Earthwatch, which recruits volunteers from around the world to assist in field research projects. Our recruitment notice in the Earthwatch catalog read ". . . Peterson needs fit and experienced wilderness backpackers to sift through the evidence in kills and wolf sign; team members strap on 20-kilo packs and hike off-trail up to 16 kilometers a day, collecting moose skeletons, examining wolf scat, and recording other prey species." Sound like fun? So far, in eight years, over 250 paying volunteers have thought so. Many of them proudly report that they've never worked so hard nor had such a great time.

In orienting eager Earthwatch volunteers, I forewarn them of the likelihood of falling. The classic off-trail fall is a study in slow-motion grace. It begins innocently enough, when a long stick gets jammed between the toe and sole of your boot. As the other end of the stick lodges in the ground and your momentum carries you forward, the impaled foot slowly rises behind you, forced up by the stick. Strapped into a heavy packframe, you are compelled to complete the fall. This experience, oft-repeated and humiliating, is an inevitable hazard of cross-country hiking on the island.

Earthwatch volunteers have become a mainstay in our summer routine, contributing both financial and field assistance. We are glad to introduce these exceptionally fine folks to Isle Royale, as they are interested and committed people from all walks of life who are united by curiosity and a desire to experience the "real" world. Earthwatchers also make terrific ambassadors for Isle Royale and its wolves.

In spite of the often arduous nature of their task, the volunteers remain surprisingly cheerful, helpful, and polite. As Earthwatcher Walter Harris put it, "If you're going to spend an in-tents week amid swamps and showers and deadfalls and downpours, it is best to do it with strangers. I know I'm much better behaved among strangers—I whine less, and I'm nothing but eager to share all effort and obligation. Among strangers, the only acceptable mood is a good one. Among strangers, things are less apt to be taken personally. Among strangers, one can have a genuine vacation from routine."

*　　*　　*

Most of the roughly 15,000 visitors who come to Isle Royale each summer seek a different sort of experience. Live moose, not bones, are a major attraction. Since both people and moose like to be in or near water in the summer, Isle Royale's many interior lakes, ponds, and bays offer great moose sighting opportunities. It is quite possible to get a close look at a moose, and this experience always inspires questions, for moose are odd-looking though well-adapted creatures.

Moose are large animals with almost-black hair, perfect for absorbing the sun's heat. They do not sweat like humans or pant like dogs and, as big as they are, they have trouble getting rid of excess body heat. Moose usually become active in the cool of the evening, just as it gets too dark for visitors' cameras. Other than swimming, the only way a moose can cool off is through simple breathing, which pulls air past moist membranes in their long nose, trachea, and lungs, and brings cooling by evaporation. As the ambient temperature climbs, moose breathe more rapidly, increasing both their metabolic rate and their need for more energy. Moose researcher Lyle Renecker in Alberta found that moose begin to increase their breathing rate when temperatures exceed just 38° F! At the lower end of the temperature scale, Renecker found that he could not reach a lower critical temperature at which moose raised their metabolic rate to produce heat, even after lowering the temperature in a metabolic chamber to -20° F and hosing down a captive moose with water.

Graduate student Timothy Ackerman studied the response of Isle Royale moose to summertime heat and found that, above 70° F, our idea of "room temperature," moose usually bedded in areas of wet ground, always in the shade. If a moose bedded in the open on a cloudy day that finally broke into sunshine, the moose got up and moved into the shade. Above 85° F, the moose sought water.

Good swimmers that are impervious to the cold, moose can survive the long swim to Isle Royale from the mainland. Four times we've recovered carcasses of white-tailed deer that washed ashore at Isle Royale,

Candy Peterson and son Trevor carefully make their way along a beaver dam.

Reconnoitering at the start of a week-long search for moose bones, this team of Earthwatch volunteers seeks a consensus on which way to go next.

Born with long legs that provide rapid escape from wolves, moose calves grow quickly during their first summer.

victims of hypothermia. On the other hand, in 1993, park visitors in a private boat found a moose in Lake Superior in early September, three miles off the north shore of Isle Royale and swimming toward the island. The visitors waited nearby to see how the moose fared, and eventually watched the moose climb out of the water onto the steep, uninviting north shore of the island. The moose appeared exhausted, and stood motionless for half an hour before recovering enough strength to walk.

Water provides critical escape habitat for moose. Females seek islands or shorelines before giving birth, and sometimes calves are left alone on a heavily browsed offshore island while the mother swims to the main island to feed.

Wolves can swim, too, but they don't seem to enjoy it much. All four reports of swimming wolves on Isle Royale came in 1980, with the wolf population at its all-time high. In one case, a moose cow and calf scrambled into Duncan Bay and began the 300-yard swim to the other side. Close behind the moose, a wolf leaped into the bay and swam after its prey, but it was soon outpaced and abandoned the effort.

Many cow moose choose to keep their offspring on small offshore islands all year long, preferring the familiar, safe landscape, despite the limited food supply, to the risks of new territory. During a mild winter, warm temperatures or frequent winds may keep ice bridges to small islands from forming, and a few feet of open water may keep away wolves and mean total security for a cow and her calf during the calf's critical first winter.

The water is not free from hazards for moose, however. Summertime observers may excitedly (and inaccurately) report a wolf-injured moose after spotting an animal with bloody wounds on its back legs. Freshwater leeches slice through the thin skin on a moose's rear legs for their required bloodmeal. The leeches drop off when the moose returns to land, but hordes of biting flies swarm around moose in midsummer, enlarging the leech sores into silver dollar-sized wounds.

Another pest that moose pick up, presumably in the water, is the parasite *Echinococcus granulosus,* or hydatid tapeworm. The eggs of this wolf tapeworm are ingested by moose and hatch into larvae, which journey to the lungs. There they develop into a cyst; inside the cysts, the larvae reproduce by the hundreds. As a moose ages, hydatid cysts accumulate and may take up half the lung volume. These walled-off cysts remain intact and inactive until the moose is killed and eaten by wolves—and moose lungs are delicacies of wolf cuisine.

While moose are merely bothered by pests like leeches, flies, and cysts, their bodies and behavior have evolved in response to predation by wolves, a more powerful agent of natural selection. The spindly legs of a newborn calf seem awkward, but young moose are precocious, able to keep up with their mothers when only a few days old. The bond between a cow and calf is strong; a calf is unable to defend itself against wolves for a full year, at least. When confronted by wolves, a cow will instinctively run to the vulnerable rear end of the calf.

When a cow is about to give birth again, the yearling is forcibly evicted from the "nest" to protect the newborn calf, which has a strong instinct to follow any nearby moving object. Life is difficult for the outcast yearlings and they tend to seek companionship with other large moving objects, occasionally people. A yearling cow spotted us one June and bounded toward us. Because we were carrying heavy packs, we couldn't do much but feel disconcerted. The yearling came close, then bounded away in fear, only to stop and look back at us with a long, patient gaze. Again she decided to check us out, approaching slowly and deliberately this time. We controlled our nerves, turned, and walked away slowly, hopeful that the yearling would not adopt us as surrogate parents. Wolves probably have an easy time with these innocent youngsters.

*   *   *

Another major objective of our summertime footwork is to determine whether the wolves seen the previous winter have denned and had pups. Wolf pups are typically born in a below-ground den by late April and are usually moved to another home, called a "rendezvous site," by late June—just about the time when moose have recovered from the stress of winter. Our search for a den presents two problems—wolves are particularly elusive in early summer, and we do not want to harass them at a critical time of the year.

Like my predecessors, I spent three summers without finding a wolf den or pups. Then, in July of 1973, Candy and I had the good fortune to locate the East Pack, which produced seven pups that summer. The wolves denned in an old, dry beaver lodge and moved in the course of the summer to four "rendezvous sites" within a few miles of the natal den. By listening to their frequent group howls, we could estimate the number of pups in the pack. What a privilege it was to learn such wolf secrets!

Once the wolves had left their den, we were able to prowl around the site and imagine what had gone on there. A moose calf had been eaten, and its well-chewed bones littered a beaten-down area in front of the den entrance. Two beaver skulls lay abandoned after suffering much wear and tear as wolf toys. A maze of tiny pup trails went everywhere, and logs were worn smooth from traffic around and through them. Seven homebound pups had left their marks. The den itself had three entrances, enlarged beaver passages, and airways. All entrances converged on a comfortable central chamber, just large enough to accommodate a nursing mother and her batch of newborn pups.

We spent many nights in late summer camped within earshot of the wolf pack. In a pack as large as this one, group howls are generated several times in a 24-hour period. One evening, while we sat quietly on an open ridge, wolf pups started barking, squeaking, and yipping in the adjacent

Breaking an infrared beam, female wolf #1071, passing along a moose trail, triggered her own photograph with an automatic camera. This wolf was trespassing in East Pack territory in July 1994. Seven months later, she was killed by the East Pack.

The debris collected from a summertime "rendezvous site" used by wolf pups included anything hard enough to endure perpetual chewing by young wolves.

Enlarged by wolves but never used as a whelping den,
this traditional fox den provided a rare alternative to
the usual wolf den in an old beaver lodge.

wooded valley. Soon five of them scampered into view, a comfortable distance away, and chased each other back and forth on the ridge. After much romping and bowling over, they disappeared down the ridge. Early the next morning, on a hunch that the wolves had relocated, Candy and I explored the ridge further, finally arriving at a high point where we could observe an open bog below. We sat down and waited for something to happen. Our luck was unbelievably good. An early morning chorus from a mob of wolves erupted right below us, and with a little maneuvering on our ridgetop, we were able to gain a clear view of their new rendezvous site.

For seven days we spent every possible moment perched on that lookout, silent and watchful. Adult wolves tended to arrive and leave in the mornings and evenings, and these were exciting times for the pups. During the early morning arrivals, the pups crowded around each adult's head. With every muscle in their bodies seemingly twitching with excitement—especially their tails and tongues—the pups jumped at the lips of their providers, an instinctive stimulus that causes adults to regurgitate whatever they're carrying in their stomachs. The adults then withdrew from the mob scene to seek peace and quiet, while the pups mopped up some nourishment.

Already, at ten weeks of age, there seemed to be an established hierarchy among the seven pups. Some led, others followed, and one was set upon by all the others. We could distinguish this pup by its small size, and it probably faced a short future. I scanned the pups carefully the next winter; only four uniformly large pups made it to the age of eight months.

We took every measure possible to avoid being detected by the wolves. We carefully avoided all their habitual trails and never cooked food in the vicinity. Insect repellent, which in those days was invariably perfumed, was out of the question, and the hum of mosquitoes in some of the tape recordings we made of wolves howling remains unforgettable 20 years later. We set up a tent in the dark and got up at sunrise to resume our watch, often after being awakened several times during the night by howling wolves.

As soon as we had found a wolf den and enjoyed success at watching wolves, we began to worry about who might learn of these secrets. Although Isle Royale visitors are a cut above the average for national parks, there are always a few unscrupulous individuals who would stop at nothing to exploit what we had seen. Photographers anxious for a scoop, naive visitors who were just enthralled with wild wolves, or even park staff could be genuine threats to wolf security. After seriously considering the option of not telling anyone (many old-timers within the Park Service claim this is the only sane course of action if you discover something special in a national park), I finally opted to divulge everything I knew to the park superintendent, Hugh Beattie, trusting him to understand my concerns. He was tickled to hear the news, and he agreed to a policy that I've followed ever since: Complete disclosure to only a few staff members charged with resource protection, with no maps drawn for the files.

Beattie's successor, Jack Morehead, wanted to institutionalize wolf security on Isle Royale, and suggested closing areas used by wolves to over-night camping, yet allowing daytime access. I was afraid this would highlight traditional areas that were important to the wolves, but Jack was way ahead of me. "We'll simply have to close enough areas so no one will know which ones actually harbored wolves," he boldly declared. And this was done.

When a few intrepid winter visitors to the island began to mingle paths with the wolves, frightening them off lakes where we could watch them from aircraft, Jack felt the park should be officially closed in winter. After all, it was unstaffed, and there was no way to get there except by expensive charter aircraft. In 20 years, only a handful of people had managed to get to the island in winter. Jack suggested this action to the regional office, and was promptly refused. However, superintendents of national parks can, by virtue of their office and responsibility, close a park in order to protect a vital resource, and Jack did just that by superintendent's orders. His action attracted little attention and few complaints, and after several years, the Park Service hierarchy went along with it. The intent of this policy was admirable: that wolves and moose would have some small piece of this planet to call their own. For a brief midwinter stint, when I and a party of researchers would descend on the place, *we* were the ones who were confined at night. Fair enough, I think.

During the 1970s, we began to learn the traditional home sites of all three of the established packs, and from their howls, we could often deduce how many pups were alive each summer. We maintained the same rigid conditions of non-interference. I wouldn't doubt, however, that the wolves knew all along that they were under watch.

One instance clarified for us how acute the wolf's sensory abilities really are. Candy and I were making our way quietly along a wooded ridge that ran parallel to a major wolf travel route leading to their den. It was mid-morning, and there was a turbulent but light head wind. We were making our way to a point beyond the den on our ridge, where we could monitor howling. But at a spot directly opposite the den, a quarter-mile from it through the woods, we were abruptly stopped by a group howl of several adults and pups. We were startled by the loudness of the howls, and I thought it might have something to do with our presence. We decided to "face the music" and see what might transpire, so we took off our backpacks and sat down on the ground, completely hidden from view by tall thimbleberry plants. After a short wait, we heard a stick snap on a beaver dam 50 yards away. Candy looked at me silently with large, unblinking eyes, and I mimicked the same face in return with furrowed brow. The wolves knew something was near, possibly a threat, and in such situations an alpha wolf or two will usually investigate.

We both sat absolutely still as the wolves began to crash rather noisily through the thimbleberry on their way directly uphill toward us. When they were a few feet away, the wolves split. One headed around us on each side, and we could now clearly see their outlines through the thimbleberry stems. This was too much for Candy, and she abruptly stood up. Both wolves bolted away noisily for a few steps, then simply vanished. I stood up and joined Candy, not too unhappy with her initiative, and the air was pungent with volatile secretions from the wolves' anal glands. They were at least as excited as we were, but they now had their information, and that was the end of it. The wolves did not abandon their den, and we continued our discreet listening, but we saw them no more that summer.

*   *   *

For Isle Royale wolves, the good times were the 1970s, when several new packs appeared and grew in size. Litters of pups were large, there was plenty to eat, and in almost every year for a decade, wolves increased in number. By 1980 there were 50 wolves in five packs; wolf researchers have not found so high a wolf density anywhere else in the world.

Much to my surprise, the wolf population bubble burst quickly. Within two years, only 14 wolves were left alive on Isle Royale. There was some evidence of social disarray. Packs were trespassing on the territory of their neighbors, and wolves were chasing and occasionally killing other wolves—classic symptoms of a wolf oversupply relative to their food. Wolf pack territories, which had contracted during years of plentiful prey, were now expanding, meaning that some wolves would have to go.

The initial portents of change, the mere tip of the iceberg, appeared early in the summer of 1979, in the form of noteworthy reports from visitors. A wolf skeleton washed ashore on a Lake Superior beach in the middle of the island, many of the bones smoothed and polished by the action of water and rocks. A wolf had died out on the ice somewhere—killed, I thought, by other wolves. Wolves escape danger by running, and they run much faster on snow-covered ice than in the island's interior.

A more telling example was uncovered by a camper exploring in the vicinity of the Daisy Farm Campground early in June of 1980. Behind

The drenched remains of a dead male wolf were hauled from an old copper mine shaft near Daisy Farm in 1980. Severely emaciated, the wolf had died of "old age" and malnutrition. Its skull proved to be the longest of any wolf skull found in the lower 48 United States.

Daisy Farm, old mining exploration pits dating from the 1840s were water-filled, and the camper found a dead wolf floating in one of these pools. We hauled it out and carried it across the harbor to our research camp, where we lay the carcass on its side and had a look. It was an adult male, but a mere shell of its former self. Many teeth were missing, and the giant piercing canines, needed to hold onto a running moose, were worn to small stubs. The end of a broken rib protruded through its hide, probably resulting from the fatal kick of a moose, but certainly not the only one. After boiling the carcass, we counted 12 broken ribs—almost half of the total, healed in small knots. A bony buildup on the wolf's skull suggested an old impact injury, similar to what we would expect from a quick moose kick that hit its mark.

It is rare for us to have an entire wolf carcass from which to decipher a cause of death, so we methodically went through each piece of evidence. The entire carcass of the wolf, dripping wet, weighed only 57 pounds—

less than two-thirds the usual weight of a male wolf. Its last reserves of fat, found in bone marrow cavities and grooves along the coronary arteries, were gelatinous and exhausted. The large muscle masses of the shoulders and thighs had withered to nothing, burned up to sustain life in spite of chronic starvation rations. Its kidneys were strangely lobed, a condition for which pathologists had no explanation. All the rest of the evidence, however, confirmed that old age and malnutrition were major factors in the wolf's death. Unable to kill prey and injured by its last contact with moose, this wolf had walked past the mine shaft, perhaps attracted by the small moose "knuckle-bone" that we found on the edge of the earthen hole. An unlucky stumble had dumped the weakened wolf into the pool of water, an ignominious end for a wild wolf.

There were other summertime indicators of food stress for the record-high wolf population. In June of 1980, a young girl was alone outside a shelter in the Malone Bay Campground, hanging a plastic tarp over the front screen wall. A scrawny-looking "dog" approached her, then withdrew when she turned around for a look. Her father knew this could not be a dog, so he captured the wolf on film and reported it to the resident park ranger. We were alerted and dispatched a crew to await the wolf's return, prepared to confront the wolf with a bit of aversive conditioning that would discourage such interaction with campers. The full story indicated a few days of easy pickings for the wolf, at the campsite of successful fishermen who had cleaned a string of lake trout. A few stops at the garbage can had prompted the wolf to abandon its fear of humans and, with no other options, to glean a subsistence living from the leavings of its age-old enemy.

A decade later, in 1990, we learned much more about the last months of decline in such a wolf, through the steady demise of wolf #550. This lone male had managed to kill moose by himself in his last full winter, but he was rarely able to enjoy the fruits of his labors. Scavengers stole large portions of his kills, and he was often chased off his own kills by the resident wolf packs. He spent most of his time on the two opposite ends of the island, evidently able to dodge the close attention of territorial packs.

When spring arrived, we found him scavenging a moose that had died from malnutrition on the nature trail behind the Windigo Ranger Station, where we caught a rare glimpse of him before he was frightened off by our approach. A few days later, a new crew of summer rangers watched him amble down the beach at Windigo in full view of a crowd on the dock, and there I found a fresh scat that suggested trouble—it contained tin foil and a mass of fish scales, plus a few colored beads that looked like fishing paraphernalia.

By midsummer, wolf #550 had learned a whole new way of life—hiding near lakeside campgrounds until people started cleaning fish, then appearing and walking slowly toward the campers while everyone quickly exited, leaving behind a pile of fish guts. With every campground occupied in August, we could track this wolf without radiotelemetry, simply by monitoring the reports of excited and concerned campers.

The wolf managed in this way until autumn, when people abandoned the island and the economy dried up for old #550. When we arrived in January, we found him dead almost on the doorstep of our winter residence, where the wolf had taken up shelter inside the hollow root ball of a fallen cedar. He probably knew we were coming and where we would live, but he expired a few days before our arrival. I was glad to be spared the dilemma of having to deal with a big, starving, near-dead friend.

After the crash of the early 1980s, the wolf population recovered temporarily to about the level it had been in the 1960s. However, an insidious change was occurring annually, of such small magnitude that it was easy to ignore. We were detecting fewer pups in summer, but the trend was all but lost in the typical "noise" of such data. What was clearer to us was a decline in the summertime howling of wolves. Astute longtime visitors to the island noticed it, and they asked me after evening interpretive talks why the wolves weren't howling anymore.

"Wolves howl together when they're happy," I replied anthropomorph- ically. "They howl when they are busy feeding many pups and coordinat- ing the activities of many pack members." That the wolves were in a new era seemed clear, even if the reasons were not. Things just weren't what they used to be.

At summer's end, with rapidly growing antlers, bull moose abandon their haunts in the island's interior in search of cow moose, lingering more often near the lakeshore.

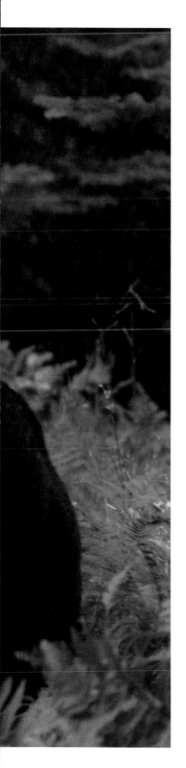

Season of Maturity

*Animals are far more fundamental to our thinking than
we supposed. They are not just a part of the fabric of
thought; they are part of the loom.*

Peter Steinhart, "Dreaming Elands," 1989

COW MOOSE HAVE CALVES, AND BULL MOOSE HAVE
antlers; the behavior of each sex has evolved out of this
difference. While the world of the cow moose revolves
around security for herself and her offspring, the
inherited strategy of successful bulls is to grow the
largest possible antlers. Fast growth rates early in life
lead to large body size at the prime of life, a prerequisite
for large antlers. Each May a new set of antlers begins
to grow, only to be shed each December. Male moose
burn their way through life, paying the price with a
shortened life span.

The only time bulls and cows spend together is
during the rut, when bulls invade the enclaves of cows
near shorelines and campgrounds, where they are safest
from the threat of wolf predation. The season opens in
early September with the shedding of skin-like "velvet"
from the new set of antlers. Both sexes become quite
vocal, and on calm nights the long, drawn-out calls of
cow moose echo across the valleys and bays, while the
"cadence grunts" of bulls advertise their searching.

For a few weeks in late September and early
October, the antlers of bulls become the focus of the
competition for the attention of cows. Anthony (Tony)

Bubenik was an authority on the behavioral significance of antlers. In Alaskan tundra, where bull moose grow the world's largest antlers and attract harems of cows, he carried a giant set of plastic antlers into the mating arena. Sporting his artificial rack, with only a rudimentary moose head on his chest and a rump patch attached to his back, Bubenik's body did not match his giant head, but moose are so interested in antlers that they pay little heed to the rest of the animal. As Tony arrived on the scene with all the proper ritualized displays, the bull moose saw they were no match for the newcomer, so they quickly exited. Cow moose, sensing that this new male was a more than adequate substitute, began to approach and court him, presenting unanticipated problems! He was forced to back down gracefully, extricating himself from the inappropriate expectations of the cows.

In the boreal forest of eastern North America, including Isle Royale, moose live in dense forest and do not gather harems. Instead, a bull finds a cow and remains with her until she is receptive, at the height of estrus. After mating occurs, the bull moves on and searches for another cow. Because female moose are rather well-synchronized, bulls may not have an opportunity to breed more than one or two cows during the rut.

Tony Bubenik was finally able to perform his antler experiments with eastern moose, but here he found bulls to be less intimidated by antler size and more likely to issue a challenge. He was forced to terminate his work with these moose, as he was clearly in danger. Mature bulls use their antlers primarily for display, and contestants approach each other stiff-legged, head and antlers slowly swaying back and forth. With a sideways glance, bulls quickly evaluate each other. As they draw closer, one usually decides to concede the match and moves on, sometimes spurred by an extra jab from the victorious bull.

When antler displays fail to determine which bull has superior qualities, it is time for contact. Competing bulls, with their heads lowered, carefully place the broad surfaces of their antlers together, intermingling the tines. Then they suddenly throw their entire weight into an intense shoving match. While in tundra areas such interactions may last for hours, forest moose like those at Isle Royale seem to have much briefer contests.

Despite short sparring matches, many bull moose on Isle Royale clearly exhaust themselves during the rut. Extra energy demands and reduced feeding force bulls to metabolize fat stored during the opulent summer months. Some researchers have suggested that bulls are so busy during the rut that they simply have no time to feed. But in a study of rutting behavior, Dale Miquelle found that Isle Royale bulls spend 45 percent of their time apparently doing nothing but standing and staring forward with an inscrutable gaze. Miquelle was at a loss to explain what, if anything, the moose were doing, except to suggest that they might be sampling the air for pheromones, the airborne cues that indicate female receptivity.

If a moose survives its second year, it has an excellent chance of reaching full maturity. Young moose continue maturing physically and behaviorally until they are about five years old, passing through what Tony Bubenik referred to as the "teen" or submature stage. He considered it essential that a proper social balance exist between teens and prime breeders that are 5 to 10 years old, for mature moose suppress premature reproductive activity in teens. Breeding is then accomplished by mature moose that have been preselected to survive the rigors of nature. Superior moose may survive another decade or more, contributing proportionately more genes to the next generation. On a grand scale, this is what drives evolution of species by natural selection.

The "fast" lifestyle for bulls continues during prime age, when all manner of activity and forage intake is funneled into growing and display-ing the most impressive antlers possible. For females, reproductive success is reflected more by individual survival; every year of life carries the possi-bility of producing another surviving calf. Cows pace themselves, while bulls seem to burn the candle at both ends. Interestingly, and probably not just coincidentally, the risk of mortality begins to increase soon after moose reach prime breeding age, or about five years old. In a sense, an adult moose becomes more expendable after it has successfully replaced itself in future generations.

Humans spend a lot of time and money trying to ignore or forestall the processes of aging and senescence. For moose, problems begin to appear at the age of seven or eight years, invariably sooner in males than females. Other than the hydatid cysts that accumulate in their lungs with age, moose maladies have a familiar ring—including arthritis, periodontal disease, and osteoporosis.

Arthritis in the lower back and hip joints can be especially debilitating, and few would doubt that crippled moose quickly fall victim to wolves.

Even in autumn, cow moose with calves seek the safety of water, which is their best protection when confronted by wolves.

Exhausted by activity during the annual rut, a bedded bull moose nods off for a rare interlude of sleep.

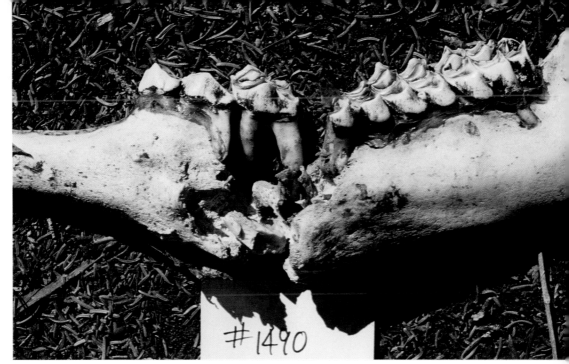

#1490

Weakened by severe infection, the lower jaw of this moose had broken in half before the animal was killed by wolves.

Arthritis is a common, age-related problem in Isle Royale moose. The normal pelvis or hip joint (top) contrasts with another revealing severe arthritis (bottom).

Periodontal infections also appear, loosening the large grinding molars as a moose gets older. Accumulated toothwear from masticating five tons of vegetation each year also compromises a moose's ability to convert green plants to energy. A slow but inexorable physical decline begins.

Osteoporosis, the thinning of bone mass, may reflect the increasing physical deficit arising from the annual production of antlers and calf moose. As they get older, moose must mine their own skeletons to be reproductively successful. For adult moose at Isle Royale, the most common age of death is 12 years. The oldest bull recovered at Isle Royale was 17 years old, and cows have lived up to 20 years.

Moose that survive to maximal age do so under periodic surveillance by wolves bent on detecting early weakness. We know little about what creates a strong constitution for a moose. Superior genetic characteristics are probably part of the story. There can be few processes of natural selection more discriminating than wolf predation, and we can expect that poor genetic combinations rarely persist in their prey. There are also important environmental influences that shape the future for individual moose. Long-term studies of Minnesota deer by Dave Mech and Michael Nelson suggest that the effects of nutritional well-being early in life may be felt for several generations. Animals that are born to well-fed parents and enjoy similarly favorable conditions tend to give birth to large and vigorous young with a high survival rate, just like people.

Senescence is both a seasonal and generational phenomenon, and understanding the latter explains the striking dependency of wolves on old moose. Young moose (calves and yearlings) are vulnerable to wolves because of their immaturity, which may be shared uniformly. The power of natural selection by wolf predation is greater when applied to the other end of the age distribution.

As the rut progresses and individual bull moose become distracted, weakened, and vulnerable, wolves become more successful at killing. Wolf kills in October often involve large bull moose with incipient pathology evident in their bones. Predators are great opportunists, and wolves travel widely to maintain surveillance of their estate. By October, wolf pups are usually large enough to begin traveling with their parents.

Autumn can be a rather spooky time to hike on Isle Royale. One senses that there is much happening in the world of moose, but the action is mostly out of sight, hidden by a veil of greenery. Nonetheless, there are sudden, unnerving appearances of bulls, as my wife and I found out on a memorable September 5th wedding anniversary. While camped in the forest, quietly downing an oatmeal breakfast, we were startled by the sound of breaking vegetation and pounding hooves. We both searched for trees to climb, while two bulls ran directly through our camp, the whites of their eyes flashing as they single-mindedly pursued their goal.

The first snows of winter may accompany the final bouts of the rutting season, marking passage to the time of the year when moose face their greatest test of survival. Bull moose with large antlers are surprisingly fragile, vulnerable to stresses imposed by their lifestyle. Some die in October of no obvious cause.

One old bull moose, radiocollared and tracked periodically for several years before dying at 15 years of age, was watched carefully during the fall rut by researcher Dale Miquelle, who invited an interested visitor to accompany him one day. After a few minutes of close observation, the visitor, a veterinarian, bet Miquelle $5 that the moose would not survive the winter, as his breathing suggested lung congestion and perhaps pneumonia. Just three weeks later the bull was found dead, his carcass still intact! This occurred several months after the bull had been plagued by a large number of winter ticks, causing hair loss, severe skin irritation, and possible harm to his immune system. Researcher William Samuels, a specialist on winter ticks and moose, reported that several moose experimentally infected by winter ticks in March died the next autumn of pneumonia. He speculated that ticks might have weakened the immune system to such a degree that, combined with the stress of the rut, a fatal pneumonia finally took hold.

In another October, before we appreciated the special vulnerability of bulls in post-rut condition, Candy and I stumbled across an intact bull moose lying dead on his side. We found ourselves a half-mile from a campground on Lake Superior that was accessible to private boats. We could see no sign of foul play, but we nevertheless suspected there might be a bullet hole on the side of the moose we couldn't examine. At any rate, bone samples were our concern.

"We'll need the skull and jaws," I declared. Candy rolled her eyes and groaned at the thought of moving 100 pounds of moose head and antlers to our boat, which was tied to the dock at the campground. The only tool I

A stand of balsam fir near Moskey Basin was severely damaged by moose browsing in 1972 (photo at left). But fifteen years later, after a decade of intensive wolf predation and a reduced moose population, the same area showed remarkable recovery (above).

This cross-section of a balsam fir tree shows suppressed growth in the middle of the stem, reflecting a period when the moose population was high. The outer rings grew rapidly when moose density was suppressed by wolf predation in the late 1970s and early 1980s.

had along was a dull sheath knife, and it was only with considerable effort that we finally managed to detach the head from the body. Using the antlers as handles, we slowly worked our way along the half-mile trail to the dock. Each time we put the head down to rest, a pool of blood drained onto the ground, so we left an obvious trail of blood from the bull's carcass.

Isle Royale was virtually deserted in October, yet we jokingly wondered how we could explain our chore to any visitors who might be standing on the dock. Indeed, when we arrived there we found another boat tied up, belonging not to a visitor but to a conservation officer from the Michigan Department of Natural Resources. I carried no identification sufficient to convince a game warden that our mission was legitimate, but as it turned out, the DNR boat was untended. We dragged the moose head across the dock, turned it over into the bilge of our boat, and quickly left the area.

It is usually best for all parties concerned if wolves find a dead moose before we do, reducing a 100-lb intact moose head to a more manageable 20 pounds or so. In 1974, after thesis-writing had kept me sedentary most of the summer, Candy and I found time for a day hike of about five miles into the 1936 burn. Out of shape, we didn't move as quickly toward our destination, a new beaver pond, as we thought we would. Just before we turned around, a bit short of our goal, we found a large bull moose that had just been killed by the East Pack. Fortunately, the skull had been meticulously cleaned by feeding wolves, but the antlers were massive. I counted on my youthful resilience to get the head to the boat, using the paired antlers as a carrying yoke across my shoulders.

Inspecting the kill site delayed us, and darkness was complete when we were yet two miles from the boat. With frequent rest stops, the final hour consisted of slowly picking our way along a park trail to the dock. Suddenly, as we walked, the East Pack broke out in a vigorous group howl from an adjacent drainage, perhaps a quarter-mile away. I wondered how discriminating a mob of wolves might be under these circumstances, and whether they could even detect me under this moose head, which appeared to be struggling down the trail upside-down and backward. Candy didn't wonder at all. She simply broke into a loud song that would leave no doubt as to our identity. There were no more rest stops until we reached the boat, tired and aching. Back at the cabin, during a late-night dinner lit by kerosene lamp, I fell asleep while eating and awoke only when my chin hit the plate.

During another October day hike, Candy and I saw the outcome of more wolf opportunism as we backtracked a string of fresh wolf tracks along a park trail. We began encountering wolf droppings full of beaver hair, and tallied these, as was our custom. Seventeen scats containing beaver hair appeared within just a few hundred yards; clearly we were on to something worthwhile.

The trail soon crossed a low drainage where, below a brown high-water mark, we found all the vegetation muddied and flattened in a down-stream direction, flash flood style. We followed the line of wolf tracks as they turned up this drainage, and soon came upon a broken beaver dam and a drained pond with a huge beaver lodge in the middle, sitting as high and dry as a beached whale. Wolf tracks were everywhere—on the surface of the pond bottom, on top of the lodge. Taking advantage of a broken dam, the wolves had evidently consumed every beaver in the colony.

*　　*　　*

Autumn is the time of heavy industry for beavers. They put up a food cache of woody twigs and stems for the winter, pack new mud over their winter lodge and dams, and lay on a final layer of body fat to help them survive through winter. In October beavers seem most active on land, felling large trees and gnawing them into lengths appropriate for transport to their pond. Twigs, bite-sized branches, and stems are organized into an underwater food cache that may rival the size of the beaver lodge. The larger the colony of beavers, the larger their food cache. Yet careful measurements of food cache size suggest that there is nowhere near enough food stockpiled to feed the entire colony. Beaver biologists believe the food cache is provided for the benefit of young beavers, or kits, while older animals live through the winter by burning stored body fat.

The tight winter lodges of beavers, and even their ponds, represent ambitious construction intended as security, and of course it is the wolf that beavers must be concerned about. One would think that beavers would be especially vulnerable to wolves during all the cutting of trees on land in October, but wolves are actually able to exploit beavers during the entire open water season, from April into November. Even in the dead of winter, if there is a thaw, wolves search out beaver colonies. Midwinter

Beaver, whose extensive water impoundments make them
the landscape architects for Isle Royale, are actively
hunted by wolves whenever there is open water.

A freshly drained beaver pond
allows wolves access to beavers
that lack a secure refuge.

Surprised one early October morning, wolves at a rendezvous site stare up at a survey aircraft.

cutting is underway, and beaver traffic is heavy along the obvious trails in the snow and near holes in the ice. All summer long, beavers are a consistent menu item for wolves, yet we know little about how wolves manage to kill them.

At Isle Royale it is uncommon for beavers to emerge from the security of the pond to cut vegetation on land in midsummer, and it seems unlikely that wolves ever venture into water after a beaver. To my knowledge, no one has actually observed wolves catching and killing a beaver, so we are left to speculate on their hunting technique. We have spent long hours listening to the beeps of radiocollared wolves at night in summer. I have been impressed with how wolves consistently travel along valley bottoms and drainages, wetlands that in all cases are maintained by beavers. These are also excellent places to find moose calves and their mothers, ever-watchful and always near water. But many times we have found that radiocollared wolves become very sedentary next to beaver ponds, staying motionless for long hours.

The one place I can think of where wolves might have a reasonable opportunity to catch a beaver in summer would be on the beaver dams themselves—those massively engineered structures consisting of rocks (at the base of the dam), logs, sticks, and mud. These dams impound the ponds in which beavers live, and the residents carefully inspect their pond security systems each night, often traveling up and down the watershed through a series of ponds. When they cross their own dams, beavers always seem to use the same runway, where they can quickly slide down on a layer of mud to a lower pond. I imagine that wolves might lie quietly on beaver dams next to a slide and simply wait. It would be a marvelous display of nervous tension—a watchful beaver making seemingly endless swimming circuits of the pond edge, nose twitching in a careful sampling of the air currents, while a wolf lies concealed and motionless, yet wound up and ready to pounce. I'm sure that subduing a 40-pound beaver is no small feat, even for a wolf, but wolves evidently have little choice. Old moose, their wintertime staple, are rarely killed during the non-winter months.

Wolf pups first encounter ice at small beaver ponds in late autumn— surely a wondrous experience for a young wolf. To find the water of a familiar pond suddenly turned solid must be a novel and irresistible invitation to experiment. Each wolf probably gets its feet wet many times before it begins to understand this new phenomenon. Wolves quickly learn to test ice by leaning out from shore and slamming a front paw on it. In January, when we can watch them, pups continue to experiment with the new ice on Lake Superior's harbors and bays.

*   *   *

Autumn is a time for plants, as well as animals, to mature. In "mast years," seed crops on many species of trees are heavy in late summer and fall, a bounty for animals such as red squirrels that must survive winter on caches of stored seeds. We learned how efficient red squirrels are when we needed seed-bearing cones of balsam fir ourselves, to use in germination experiments that were being conducted by graduate student Brian McLaren.

Squirrels appear to be the best judges of seed maturity; when the first fir cones started falling on the cabin roof at 6 a.m., we declared the season open for our own seed collections. Many times we could simply scurry around on the ground beneath a fir tree while a squirrel worked above, collecting some of the squirrel-cut cones. We obtained others through the ingenuity of our son Trevor, at the time a 12-year-old Rube Goldberg who helped Brian fashion a cone-cutter out of a two-pronged meat fork, a razor blade, and a net for a catchment device—all attached to the end of a long pole with plenty of duct tape.

Brian used these cones to help answer the question, "Why does balsam fir look so different on the east and west ends of Isle Royale?" In the 1980s millions of young balsam fir trees, the forest of the future, emerged in the understory on the east end of the island, while sapling fir trees on the west end remained so heavily browsed by moose in winter that they were unable to escape and become real trees. (The middle of the island was burned over in 1936, and today has little balsam fir.) This puzzle has many pieces, one of which is the much higher density of germinating seeds and young fir trees on the east end, where soils are thin and trees are often blown over. This results in more rotting wood and moss, good media for germination.

There is an equivalent volume of wood locked up in tree biomass at both ends of Isle Royale, but at the west end the trees are older, larger, and spaced more widely than at the east end. Historic disturbance of the forest on the east end led to optimal conditions for balsam fir a century later. Yet it took a period with fewer moose, provided by heavy wolf predation in the 1970s, to release fir trees from moose herbivory and let them grow into the forest canopy. Brian's studies of tree rings in balsam fir indicated that west end fir saplings also grew better when wolf numbers were high in the late 1970s, but even so, the saplings were unable to escape. There were still too many moose feeding on too few trees.

By the year 2010, a remarkable change will have occurred in the forest canopy at Isle Royale's west end. The narrow, pointed spires of mature fir trees that now grace the shorelines and bays will have largely disappeared from the west half of Isle Royale. The balsam fir is a relatively short-lived tree with a life span of about one century, and all west end fir trees grew up before moose colonized Isle Royale. Studies of tagged trees have revealed that about five percent of these trees die each year. Often, they are snapped off by the fearsome storms of November that sweep across Lake Superior, signaling the twilight of annual growth and renewal, and the beginning of a drama of survival.

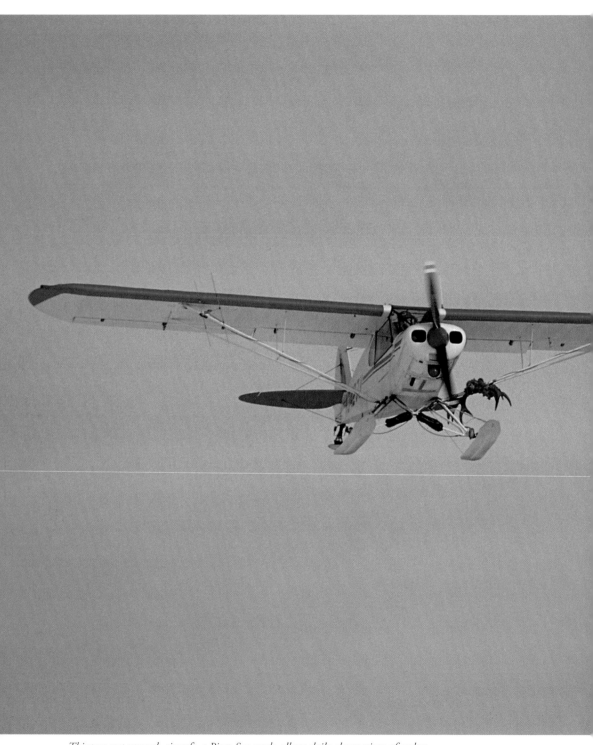

This two-seat research aircraft, a Piper Supercub, allows daily observations of wolves and access to most of Isle Royale in winter. Securely lashed to the wing strut is a moose skull with antlers, being ferried back to the winter base camp at Windigo.

Among the Ravens

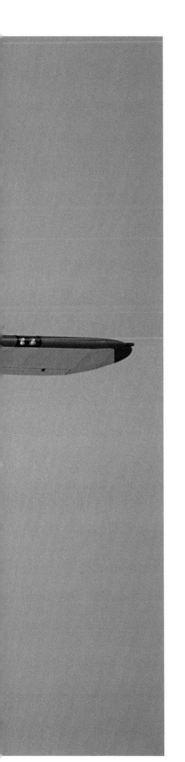

But nature is a stranger yet;
The ones that cite her most
Have never passed her haunted house
Nor simplified her ghost.

To pity those that know her not
Is helped by the regret
That those who know her, know her less
The nearer her they get.
        Emily Dickinson, 1877

MY FIRST LOOK AT A WILD WOLF, WHILE CERTAINLY memorable, was also a little discouraging. I was in an aircraft in January of 1971, a passenger flying over Isle Royale. Don Murray, the veteran winter pilot of 13 years, had located a wolf pack on a new kill in a cedar swamp, and I was now the official observer. Anticipating my interest, he brought the plane around in a sickeningly tight turn and spotted some landmarks that would help us come back for a closer look on another pass.

The next several minutes seemed to last forever. My stomach quickly tied itself in a heavy knot. The only thing I saw, when I could open my eyes, was a solid wall of dark green trees that appeared to be straight ahead. Anxious to help, Don hollered "Right there!" over the roar of the engine every time we passed the wolves. Reswallowing my breakfast, all I could do was hang on and nod my head, as if everything was perfectly clear.

Actually, I don't remember if I even saw a wolf that first day, but I do recall thinking that the next three years would be very long indeed. It was best to keep focused on a simple goal—to learn as much about wolves as the average raven on Isle Royale.

*   *   *

To understand the beast, one must first be able to find it. Everything I needed to know in order to locate wolves from aircraft, before the electronic age, I learned from Don Murray. I quickly realized that no one could follow a wolf track from an aircraft better than he. Using radio collars to locate animals was experimental when the study began, and such devices weren't permitted at Isle Royale until the 1980s, so the ability to "read" and follow wolf tracks was indispensable to the research effort. Don managed this by simply turning the plane over on its side and circling tightly, all the while watching for subtle clues on the ground. Tracking wolves while spinning over the forest canopy was a slow, agonizing process that could make anyone sick, and sometimes 25 miles of circles were required to make a mile of forward progress.

Eventually I managed to control my intense nausea by taking photographs from the plane. When I was poking a heavy telephoto lens out an open window in sub-zero temperatures, the simple task of focusing the camera with half-frozen fingers forced me to open my eyes and ignore my stomach. I slowly began to see the small cues that Don used in tracking. After a few years and hundreds of flight hours, I occasionally discovered something important a split second before Don did.

Don's ability to follow wolf tracks using aircraft was absolutely amazing to me, and when I searched his bag of tricks I was somewhat disappointed to learn that the essence of tracking wolves from a plane was simply experience. Telling the difference between fox and wolf tracks (or, initially, even moose tracks), determining which way the wolves were traveling, learning where to look next when tracks were lost, and knowing when to persevere and when to quit—I would have to learn all these things, and Don became my most valuable teacher.

What had started as a stint as a Ph.D. student became a long-term commitment in 1975 when, with Durward Allen's blessing on the occasion of his retirement, I took over as director of the study and moved as close as possible to the island—to Michigan Technological University in the state's Upper Peninsula. From 1976 to 1979, I willingly doubled my load by conducting another study of wolves and moose on Alaska's Kenai Peninsula for the U.S. Fish and Wildlife Service. Kenai provided valuable experience with another wolf-moose system, and I learned techniques of wolf capture and radiotelemetry that would someday be needed at Isle Royale. But each winter brought me back to the island for 50 days.

In 1979 came the day I had long dreaded—the day Don Murray announced that, after 21 years, he would have to quit. Acting on Murray's final piece of advice, by virtue of which I am still alive, I located and signed on another veteran pilot.

Don Glaser had known Don Murray and flown for him periodically for more than a decade. In many ways, these two gentlemen (a label that will bring a chuckle to both) were cut from the same mold. Piloting the plane was second nature to them, and both had the wide-ranging skills necessary to function safely in a remote setting.

While Don Murray was a wolf tracker without equal, Don Glaser is a moose specialist with an inexhaustible supply of energy. He is not the sort to quietly curl up with a book when grounded on a snowy day; he invariably seeks out a project and leaves his mark. With the energy of two or three ordinary people, he is at his best when constructively occupied, and he has made more than a few important discoveries.

One day in 1981, Don Glaser and I landed his ski plane on the ice alongside the island's north shore, in order to pick up bones from a wolf-killed moose. Even though this scenario has been played out hundreds of times during the annual winter studies, there are always clues to decipher. While I busied myself at the kill site, Don uttered his usual "I'll take a look around" and disappeared. Soon he returned and, almost unable to contain himself, whispered, "What'll you give me for a wolf's tail?" When he told me it was still connected to a wolf, I promised him anything just to break the suspense. He motioned for me to be quiet and follow him.

A short way down the shore, in the shelter of an overhanging tree, a wolf was indeed curled up in a ball. We were quite certain that the wolf was dead, but just in case, we edged toward it on our hands and knees. Don anxiously led the way, while I snapped photos and waited for a

*Pilot Don Murray secures
the plane for the night with
ropes buried in the ice.*

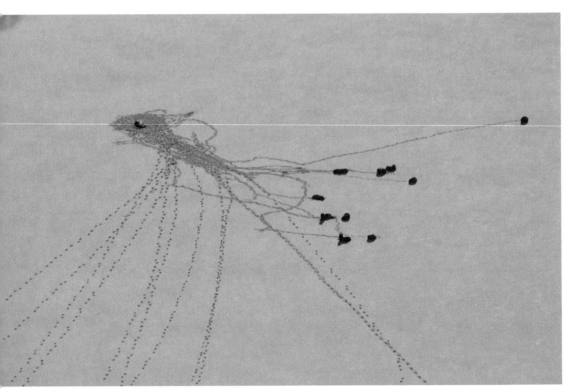

*Tracks told the story on a lake surface where the resident East Pack chased down and attacked
a single wolf. Harrassed and suppressed during the attack, the wolf lay still and was thought
dead until researchers stopped to recover it. The wolf then quickly got up and ran off.*

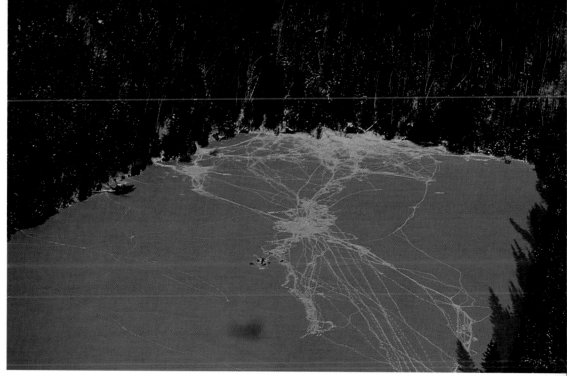

The telltale tracks of a large wolf pack near a kill help researchers toward their goal—a continuous record of the travels and kills of each wolf pack.

Pilot Don Glaser found this limp wolf carcass bedded near a wolf-killed moose in 1981. The wolf was a victim of old age and malnutrition.

once-in-a-lifetime encounter with a wolf. Don finally crept close enough to nudge it gently with the handle of our hatchet, and we braced for some sort of explosion. Alas. The wolf was a lifeless ball of fur, dead for an hour or two.

Realizing what a scientific prize this was, Don immediately set his mind to the task of fitting me, the still-limp wolf, and several large bags of moose bones into the back of the plane—an area three feet long and 20 inches wide. There was some suggestion from Don that there might not be enough room for me! At least his priorities were in order. Freezing destroys cell walls and renders internal tissues useless to pathologists, so we were elated to find this warm specimen, the first such in 35 years.

The wolf had starved to death after a long and useful life. Active to the last, it had just arrived to scavenge the moose kill, and only its tracks, which revealed a tentative, short gait and dragging feet, indicated anything amiss. Internally, the wolf was a veritable museum piece of pathology, with a half dozen old fractures in its ribs, several meters of intestinal tapeworms, and a vertebral column stiffened by arthritis. Because it was both unfrozen and dead from old age, this carcass was doubly rare and valuable.

*   *   *

If you hang around experienced pilots enough, especially when the weather is bad and time is passing slowly, the conversation will eventually turn to the subject of "close calls." Don Glaser will casually relate any one of a half-dozen tales of forced landings with a dead engine, but none of these happened at Isle Royale. After 35,000 hours in light aircraft, almost all of them in the "bush," there isn't much he hasn't seen.

Don Murray is apt to bring up a story from 1978, one I remember well because I was a back-seat passenger. At the time, I had heard Don describe how, under certain weather conditions, snow can fall from a clear sky, but I remained politely skeptical until the day I saw it for myself. In the morning, we took off from our base camp at Washington Harbor and headed for the other end of the island, 40 miles away. Because we traveled in a plane whose top speed was about 90 mph, and which carried no more than three hours of fuel, we always kept a close eye on the western horizon, where "home" was. Don's instrument panel was modest, to say

Don Murray ponders how to fit the skull of an antlered moose inside our two-seat aircraft.

The research plane, parked on glare ice during a midwinter thaw that brought research to a standstill. These foggy conditions can last for several days on Isle Royale.

*Stranded on glare ice with a frightened calf, a frustrated cow moose is unable
to move her calf to safety. Don Glaser inspected the scene, then left the area.
The moose were able to leave 24 hours later, after a fresh snowfall.*

Pilot Don Murray was headed home in 1972 with a load of bones from a moose skeleton found along the shoreline.

the least, so we flew strictly by VFR ("visual flight rules"). In short, we could fly only where we could see.

On that particular day the sky was hazy, but the sun shone bright with promise. Thirty miles out, however, we glanced back and grew uncomfortable at the sight of an obscured horizon. There was no need to explain, especially over the engine's roar; Don just shook his head, spun the plane around, and headed back. The sun was still shining, but I agreed that it was better to be safe than sorry.

At 15 miles out on the return trip, the first snowflakes began to fall, glistening in the still-bright sunlight. Twelve miles from home, we hit a wall of snow so thick and dark that we immediately dropped to treetop level to stay oriented. Don flew carefully along a narrow ridge, veering when necessary to avoid tall white pines, but conditions grew worse. Finally, unable to proceed and with nowhere to land, Don used his final option. He dove down off the ridge to the island's north shore, which rose steeply 300 feet straight out of the jumbled ice of Lake Superior. Following the shore would take us home, but we were soon just a few feet off the rough ice. The shore was situated just off our left wingtip, barely visible as a vague, light gray line against an all-white background. This was Don's only visual clue, and it was our last chance.

There was no turning back; a pivot would take us either into the steep cliffs or out over the all-white ice floes of Lake Superior, where visibility was zero. Fortunately, Don knew every irregularity in the shoreline for the final ten miles, and he became quiet in intense concentration. Ignoring my own pounding heart, I kept my mouth shut and tried to keep track of the all but invisible shoreline.

Finally we rounded the end of the island and entered three-mile-long Washington Harbor, with our base camp at its head. We immediately felt better, as smooth ice rather than a minefield of ice chunks lay beneath us. Still hugging the shore, we started the final shallow turn to land in our customary track. Tilted just a few degrees, our right ski glanced lightly off the snow surface and we became acutely aware of how low we had been flying. Don "felt" his way down the final few inches, and we came to a smooth stop at the end of the beloved dock of our base camp. The dock was 90 feet long, and we could not see its other end. After a characteristic shrug and an extended string of exclamatory remarks, Don climbed out of his seat and stood quietly on the ice, looking for something familiar through the huge snowflakes. Flooded with relief, we were soon chattering about, of course, the weather. As usual, Don Murray was right. Snow can indeed fall from a clear sky.

*   *   *

Anyone who has had the privilege of watching wolves in the wild knows something of the special relationship that exists between wolves and ravens. Ravens in winter rely heavily on the bounty of wolf kills, and the two species often travel in concert, prodding each other. The wolves watch for a raven with its guard down, and the ravens seem to take every opportunity to annoy the wolves, especially when the animals are resting—after all, sleeping wolves don't kill moose.

There is more than playfulness between wolves and ravens. Ravens make their living by scavenging wolf-killed moose (the fresher the better), and as we start the day by flying along wolf tracks, we often overtake ravens doing exactly that. When wolves pause, the birds also stop, roosting in trees or swooping to the ice where they can watch and harrass the wolves at close range. Once disturbed, wolves generally resume travel, which is precisely what benefits the ravens. In addition, few wolf scats deposited on open ice escape the selective recycling provided by foraging ravens.

Obviously, wolves are of significant benefit to the ravens; but it is possible that the relationship is not completely one-sided. Single wolves on their own, like ravens, are professional scavengers, and have no doubt found food by listening for the noisy birds on a carcass.

Might wolves also use ravens as scouts, to help them find living moose that are vulnerable to attack? While tantalized by this possibility, I have not personally seen convincing evidence that ravens actually help wolves hunt. Years ago, Don Murray and I watched a pack hunting upwind in the island's interior (according to Don's wisdom, wolves are hunting seriously *only* when moving upwind). The wolves traveled along one side of a narrow alder lowland. A short distance ahead, on the other side of the alders, stood a cow moose and calf on alert, staring in the direction of the wolves. As I watched the two moose through binoculars, a raven suddenly flew into sight, vigorously flapping its wings above the moose. I fully expected to see

*A raven quickly takes off
after taunting the wolves
resting nearby.*

the wolves cut through the alders and confront the moose that had been advertised so well by the raven, but they maintained their former course and passed less than 100 yards from their favorite prey.

Years later, we watched a raven flying back and forth over a moose on a broad upland ridge in advance of an approaching lone wolf. The raven then flew to the wolf and flapped a few times over its head. If it was trying to tell the wolf about the moose it had spotted, either its message was garbled or the wolf wasn't interested. The moose, perhaps aware that ravens and wolves often go together, beat a hasty retreat.

*   *   *

While wolves have lived with ravens for eons and accept being "hounded" with equanimity, they had to be taught to tolerate our huge, artificial raven. One of Dave Mech's greatest worries during that first Isle Royale winter in 1959 was that the wolves would be afraid of the study plane. Obviously, students of animal behavior must not frighten their subjects.

The wolves that had colonized the island could have been familiar with guns and airplanes, for the two came as a package on the mainland. In midcontinent North America, aerial wolf hunting was a brief phase in

Ravens, the constant companions of hunting wolves in winter, share in both the hunt and the spoils.

A raven stops to consume wolf scat under the watchful eyes of a well-fed wolf.

wolf-human history, however, and the Isle Royale wolves quickly learned that the noisy red and white bird was harmless.

There have been exceptions, however. In 1972, an uninvited plane visited the island before our annual winter study and harrassed the wolves. It took us weeks to renew our acquaintance with the wolves and to restore their confidence. For us, the key is to be absolutely predictable, from the animals' standpoint. Only then do they ignore us and go about their business. We try our best to be consistent in where we live, where we park the plane at night, our engine speed and flight pattern, and the altitude of our survey flights. We generally fly close to wolves for photos or observations only under very specific conditions—when we can glide past them over open ice with the engine idling as quietly as possible.

Sometimes we wish the wolves weren't so totally oblivious to the airplane circling overhead. While moose rarely close their eyes for more than a few seconds, wolves take prodigious naps and spend a large part of their lives sleeping. Every time we observe a wolf, it is important to identify which wolf it is. Isle Royale wolves are all similarly colored, and their tails offer the most distinguishing characteristics. For us to see a wolf's tail, of course, the animal must be up and about.

I recall when Don Glaser and I tracked a pair of wolves that had just killed a lone wolf. We were anxious to confirm whether these wolves were the territorial pair that "owned" that particular part of the island. The wolves were sleeping soundly on a lakeshore. With obvious glee, Don announced, "I'll get 'em up!" For the next ten minutes, he tried every noisy aerial maneuver imaginable, right over their heads. But not even a head was raised, and we were forced to give up.

In the role of observers, we go to great lengths to avoid becoming active participants in the wolf-moose drama. Don Murray liked to speculate on whether we could lead hunting wolves to vulnerable moose, as I think ravens might. We both agreed that it would probably work, but also that "Doc (Durward Allen) would kill us," so we carefully distanced ourselves from hunts during those critical seconds when the wolves closed in on a moose.

I must confess, however, that I have occasionally felt compelled to become a minimal participant in a wolf's affairs. Don Glaser and I were once keeping special watch on a certain lone wolf that often risked encounters with territorial packs in order to scavenge a meal. This wolf would steal into the island's interior and feed quickly on a resident pack's kills, then go far out on the ice of Lake Superior to sleep, evidently out of harm's way. One afternoon we found our sleeping loner on a piece of ice that was half a square mile in size. The floe was freshly broken away and had been drifting parallel to the secure shelf ice along the island's north shore, but it was now snagged temporarily on a shoreline projection. Rather than letting an unsuspecting wolf float off to certain doom, we felt obliged to wake it up and let it decide whether it was in danger.

After we made a single low pass, the wolf's head came up, and it sleepily watched us circle around a second time. The wolf calmly looked at the island's shore and then, with its head back down, it lay flat on its side, stomach distended and legs stretched out. It obviously did not wish to be disturbed. As expected, the wolf sailed off into Lake Superior, resting in peace on its private ice floe, and we never saw it again. The wind switched a couple of days later, and we like to think that the wolf made landfall again on the island.

*   *   *

I often wonder how much the wolves understand about our operation. Generations of Isle Royale wolves have observed the annual cycle of researchers coming in January, flying around in a small plane, and leaving abruptly a few weeks later—rather like seasonal migrants. We come out only in daylight, usually in favorable weather. Like ravens, we are diurnal and spend a lot of time following wolf trails. Our occasional low passes are similar to the teasing of low-flying ravens, and I suspect that the wolves would like to catch us.

Without fail, we roost at night in the same buildings, which the wolves carefully avoid. They allow us a half-mile or so of exclusive space around our winter bunkhouse, and only three times in 25 years have I seen them cross the line into this human-occupied arena. Each incident happened at night, when intense curiosity overcame their fear. The first such trespass occurred the night after we brought a dead wolf from the other end of Isle Royale, then hauled it by sled up the hill from the plane to the carpenter's shop. Here, we unceremoniously skinned and dissected the carcass of the animal, which had been killed by other wolves. That

*A red fox takes up the midnight watch
at our bunkhouse door in winter,
usually a refuge from wolves.*

*A sleeping wolf on the ice illustrates the
relaxed response of Isle Royale animals
to the familiar research aircraft.*

night, while we slept, a single wolf walked past the bunkhouse door over to the shop, then continued into the woods beyond. This could be more than a coincidence, I thought at the time.

Years later, we recovered another dead wolf. This time we kept the animal doubly sealed in plastic during its trip to the carpenter's shop, then unwrapped it and left it intact on a bench overnight. In the morning we once again followed the track of a single wolf past the bunkhouse and the shop door. To me this seemed like pretty good evidence that wolves have an unbelievably acute sense of smell, and that the Isle Royale wolves were keenly aware of our presence.

The third time, I made it easy for them. I dropped the bagged wolf at the door of our bunkhouse, then dragged it across the snow to the shop. You can probably guess what happened that night.

One might think that Isle Royale wolves can anticipate our behavior rather reliably; certainly there is evidence of this. One of Durward Allen's regular activities in the 1960s and 1970s involved "collecting," by rifle, a moose each year—usually about two to three days after our arrival. The moose was weighed, measured, and dissected. Appropriate specimens were collected, and the carcass was then dragged across the harbor ice to a point of land beneath a large dead pine. Without fail, the West Pack came within a day to accept our largess—attracted by the calls of ravens, or so we thought. The ground observations of wolves thus obtained were invaluable.

Yet it was not just the raven's vocal symphony that brought the wolves in, as we were to discover one year when there was no carcass on the harbor ice. Durward's last "collection" took place in 1975, during his final winter study, and I managed to keep the tradition going in 1976. By the next year, however, the moose population had hit such a low level that we could scarcely find a moose near our base camp. For the first time in the wolves' memory, a free moose was not associated with the arrival of researchers, and no ravens trumpeted the availability of a carcass. Nevertheless, three days after our arrival, we found eight wolves of the West Pack curled up in a tight cluster beneath the dead pine. All the next day—for 24 hours—they waited for the annual ritual to be enacted, but no moose appeared. Indeed, for the next 15 years no moose were collected. During this time, wolves never again graced us with an extended presence on the harbor.

Any doubts about the wolves' possible insights into our behavior were removed for me in a single stunning demonstration late one afternoon as we routinely began our final check on the wolves before calling it a day. The West Pack had just left a kill and traveled three miles across glare ice to rest on a point of land. One straggler remained at the kill, still feeding. This wolf finally finished and headed along the pack's old trail, which led away from the pack's current location. We circled this trotting wolf for several minutes in order to identify it, then flew straight to the West Pack for another look. We circled the pack a few times and headed back to the single wolf, which, to our amazement, had left the other trail and was coming to join the pack. From tracks, we could see that this wolf had turned and begun traveling directly along our flight line, diagonal to all topographical features and perpendicular to the wind, heading straight for the sleeping pack. Within minutes, the single wolf was reunited with the pack in a joyous greeting. Surely, I thought, that wolf had used the plane to find its fellows. We were glad to be of service.

*   *   *

When on the ground, we try to dissociate ourselves from the plane as much as possible, to prevent the wolves from developing an aversion for the vehicle. We avoid landing near kills if any wolves are present; we never land or take off within sight of wolves; and we try never to be seen getting into or out of the plane. All aerial maneuvers near wolves are made within their sight, to avoid surprises. The wolves trust us completely, but only when we are in the plane.

Wolves usually ignore the plane, but they react differently to the human form on the ground. In fact, anything remotely resembling an upright human seems to trigger flight. I recall watching two pups, almost fully grown, traveling together over the ice. As they rounded the end of a small island, a single adult moose stood a quarter-mile ahead on the frozen lake, facing directly away from them. From that angle, the rear end of a moose looks quite like a human—about six and a half feet tall, with two very long legs. The two wolves took one look, turned, and bolted away at high speed, as if they'd just seen me!

While the Isle Royale wolves are clearly terrified of people, they seem to have forgotten why. Their collective memory of firearms has apparently vanished. This explained the odd behavior of a lone wolf that Don Murray and I once inadvertently surprised at a kill, just a short distance inland from the rugged Lake Superior shore. We had flown over the kill and had not seen any wolves, so we landed on the ice, taxied noisily to a stop directly opposite the kill, and climbed out with our packs open for more specimens. We were totally taken aback as a wolf dashed from shore just 50 yards away, ran out onto the smooth ice surface, then stopped to watch us closely. The wolf was edgy, ready to flee at the slightest stimulus. To stand in the open within easy rifle range would be a foolish response for a mainland wolf, but to a wolf naive about firearms, there is no danger that cannot be outrun—and that is exactly what the wolf was poised to do.

The topic of wolves' fear of humans recently came up in a conversation with Erich Klinghammer, an ethologist who specializes in wolf behavior. He visited a captive group of wolves in Europe—wolves that originated from German, Italian, and North American stock, yet were all raised together. Wolves of different origins responded differently to his howling, and Erich decided that there might be a strong genetic component to the way wolves respond to people, concluding that "natural" selection has favored shy wolves. Where wolves have been persecuted for centuries, or even millennia, they are extremely frightened of people; wolves that exhibited bold tendencies were eliminated long ago.

After 40 years on Isle Royale, wolves continue to be as afraid of people as they were when their ancestors arrived. Several generations of Isle Royale wolf pups have been born, typically in dens as far from people as possible, and young wolves probably do not see humans until they are well beyond their eight- to ten-week socialization period. It's likely that, through culture (non-genetic transmission of information), wolf parents instill in their pups stern advice about avoiding humans.

"Once the wolf is used to Yellowstone, two or three generations later, when they aren't getting shot, they'll lose their fear of humans." This, an excerpt from the debate in the 1990s about introducing wolves to Yellowstone, is sadly reminiscent of early anti-wolf sentiment at Isle Royale 40 years ago. Wolves will kill off all the moose, the argument goes, and then they'll start attacking people.

It is a subject of enduring interest that, on Isle Royale, they did not.

A wolf pack chases a moose unsuccessfully through 15 inches of snow. After a mile the moose turned and faced the wolves, then walked off unmolested following a brief face-off.

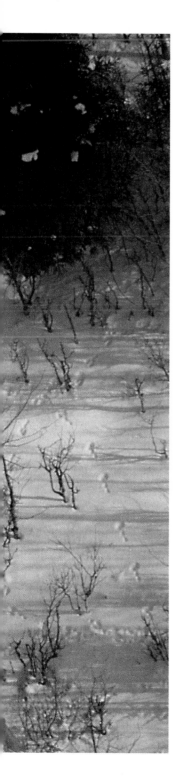

Dance of Death

Whether wolf and prey act according to some mutual understanding, or whether they only unconsciously participate in a fundamental drama, is something we shall probably never know. All we do know, staring up at the paintings of game animals on the cave walls at Lascaux, is that the belief that there was more to hunting than killing, and that dying was as sacred as living, was not something that one day just fell out of the sky.

Barry Lopez, *Of Wolves and Men*, 1978

IN NATURE, DEATH IS MERELY AN ACT IN LIFE'S DRAMA, and the wolves of Isle Royale perform their appointed role as agents of death for moose, beaver, fox (sometimes), and other wolves (rarely). The wolf itself, as top predator in this cast of characters, most often dances alone with death. Whether it is preferable to be killed or to die by other means is the sort of question that only people ask. Perhaps this chapter will provide some insight into the reality of death for members of other species.

One might think that watching wolves hunt and kill moose is the daily fare of Isle Royale researchers, but since we need daylight to watch wolves, and they hunt at night, we rarely observe the predator-prey system we study. During more than 20 winters, I have seen a couple of hundred wolf-moose confrontations, ten of which resulted in a kill. Probably a large part of the mystique surrounding wolves is their nocturnal nature; when we see a pack of wolves stretched out on the ice, their bellies distended, we know what they were up to just hours before, but we must follow their tracks, find clues, and add our own speculation to complete the picture.

Durward Allen once remarked, "The only thing a predator requires of its prey is that it hold still." The wolves' immediate objective, in full chase after a running moose, is to bring the huge juggernaut to a standstill, for then the job is 90 percent complete. The options for accomplishing this, even for a carnivore as powerful as a wolf, are surprisingly limited.

A major challenge for a wolf involves finding a place to get a grip on its gigantic prey. The moose's massive body has large, rounded contours, and the legs and head offer the only vulnerable points. Front legs are carefully avoided, as these are the moose's most formidable weapons. Oddly enough, the rubbery, cartilaginous snout of a moose is occasionally caught by canine teeth and clamped between the substantial jaw muscles of wolves. There is a risk in this approach, since a moose can lift a 90-pound wolf completely off the ground and toss it about.

By far the most common point of wolf attack is the rear end, especially the upper hind legs. While this is the "best" approach for a wolf, there are inherent difficulties. From my field notes in 1990:

"Early in February the East Pack, consisting of an alpha pair and three pups, entered a thicket of trees near Lake Mason. A moose soon ran out of the thicket, followed by the alpha male, lunging through the snow just inches behind. With one ambitious and seemingly reckless leap, the male grabbed and locked his jaws on a back leg of the running moose. Hanging on was no small feat, because of the piston-like movements of the moose's leg, and the alpha male was jolted up and down through the air like a rag doll.

"As the moose slowed to weave its way through another clump of trees, the alpha female was able to assist her mate. Now the moose was slowed down by two wolves, one attached leech-like to each hind leg. The moose continued lunging ahead for another four minutes, mainly on the strength of its front legs. As the moose came to a halt, the three pups caught up, but they carefully distanced themselves from the pounding hooves of the moose. The moose collapsed onto its sternum, keeping its head up to watch the wolves and kicking out with its rear legs, desperately trying to regain its footing. The two adult wolves worked quickly now, tearing at the moose's rump. Blood appeared in the snow beneath the moose. The pups, still fearful of the thrashing moose, continued to watch from a safe distance.

"With a sudden lunge the moose regained its feet, the alpha male still clinging tightly to one leg. The moose pummeled the wolf with rapid-fire kicks of its other rear leg. (Little wonder that old wolves at Isle Royale have suffered fractured scapulae, cracked skulls, and broken ribs!) The moose lashed out at the alpha female, who danced just out of reach in front of the moose. Action now reached a frenzy, the blood-soaked male refusing to yield his hold while the moose whirled back and forth in a vain effort to trample the alpha female. The pups, clearly frightened, clung to safety behind a circle of trees.

"Unable to gain a hold up front, the alpha female finally rejoined the male, and, side by side, each held tightly to the rear of the moose. The wolves were dragged over logs and thrown against trees as the moose whirled around, but they maintained their hold. Only when the moose actually sat on the wolves did they let go, to quickly shift their hold. Over the next few minutes, the moose slowed and finally went down again onto its sternum. With its head up, panting heavily, the moose frequently glanced back at the wolves. But gradually its lunges became feeble, and finally the rear legs could kick no more."

When confronted by wolves, a moose may back up against an overturned tree, a rock, or anything else that might protect its backside. Conifer cover and cedar "swamps," low-lying forests with a tangle of northern white cedar in all stages of growth and decay, seem to offer the best protection at Isle Royale—especially in late winter, when weakened moose and crusted snow give wolves some advantage. For moose, this is evidently a successful strategy every time but the last; we are uncommonly successful at finding skeletons of moose in cedar swamps.

An old forest with lots of downed trees also allows a moose to "comb" the wolves from its backside by running or twirling around and violently throwing them against trees. This behavior helps explain the broken ribs often found in the skeletons of old wolves on Isle Royale.

*   *   *

Nature does not abandon a dying moose. In the brains of all mammals, small amounts of morphine-like compounds that block pain receptors are released. In the 1970s physiologists named these chemicals endorphins and found that they are released in stressful situations—those classical "fight or flight" scenarios such as I've just described.

Writing on the evolution of endorphin response, scientist and philosopher Lewis Thomas pointed out that pain can be a useful warning, as when one picks up a hot object. However, in a situation perceived as a life-threatening emergency, pain would distract from the singularly important objective of saving one's life. So there might be an adaptive advantage in the temporary elimination of pain when an animal is facing a serious threat.

Before the discovery of endorphins, we talked about a mortally wounded moose as being in a "state of shock." Standing motionless with its head down and its eyes forward, the animal appears to be in a trance. Wolves will often cease attack at this point and simply wait for the inevitable. The moose dares not lie down; it cannot move about to feed (regular food intake is important for a ruminant animal); and its vital signs weaken. Massive release of endorphins can actually lead to a heart attack, and this may explain how some moose die, for their wounds after a wolf attack can be surprisingly superficial. At other times, the final wait goes on for days, and wolves may simply lie down and watch the wounded moose. The longest standoff I've seen, which happened in 1978 with the entire West Pack of wolves in constant attendance, lasted for seven days. The moose remained standing for the entire time.

*   *   *

In describing the subtle transfer of information when wolf meets moose, author Barry Lopez referred to a "conversation of death." This critical interaction is not often seen by humans, and wolves employ subtle animal senses, so there is much room for speculation. A wolf's nose adds an extra dimension to the world that we cannot appreciate. Here is a creature that can stand and examine a bare patch of ground near a trail junction for fully five minutes, investigating and interpreting who or what has passed. Perhaps wolves can distinguish a vulnerable moose by *smell,*

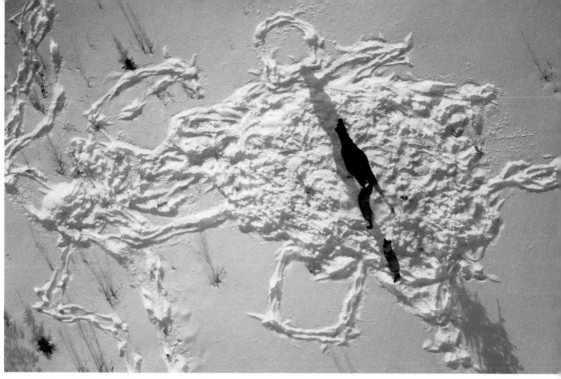

A 30-minute struggle enabled two wolves to bring down a yearling moose that was caught far from protective cover.

A mortally wounded moose calf is tended by the East Pack in 1994.

either through pheromones that might betray the uneasiness of the prey or through indicators of senescence or vulnerability. When I thaw out the mandibles of wolf-killed moose that had tooth or periodontal infections, I often find impacted bits of browse lodged in holes or lesions between their teeth. This may amount to half a teaspoon of old, partly digested twigs with a characteristically unpleasant odor that may gag a person on first exposure. Any odor that *I* can detect must be quite obvious to wolves at a great distance.

In winter, fully one-third of the wolf kills on Isle Royale are calf moose, easily distinguished as prime targets.

Through experience, I've learned the strength of the cow-calf bond in moose, and the danger it poses for those who come between a cow and her calf. In a February 1973 flight we observed a lone calf moose lying on its sternum on the ice next to the north shore of the island. Don Murray landed on the nearest smooth ice, a mile down the shore, and Durward Allen and I went to investigate. Durward carried the "collecting rifle" and, after finding the calf helpless and unable to move, he used the gun to put it out of its misery and to provide an intact moose for examination. After assisting with the initial diagnosis and dismembering of the calf, Durward left with the rifle to continue his flight, while I proceeded with knives and bone saw to dissect the calf, which had suffered a spinal cord injury in a fall off the icy north shore.

The quiet routine of my investigation was broken by a steady crunching in the snow onshore. In a momentary panic I realized that a cow moose was returning to check on her calf. I dropped the knives and ran as fast as I could along the shore, managing to scamper into an overhanging tree just before the pursuing cow thundered to a stop at its base.

After what seemed an eternity of waiting the cow moose walked back to her calf, now in pieces with organs strewn on the ice. I was shocked to see the cow moose begin eating the stomach contents of her calf; I was also distressed to realize that my stay in the tree might be extended considerably. When Don and Durward finally flew back for a look, they quickly saw my predicament. Don thought he could haze the cow from the area by repeatedly "buzzing" her in a series of low passes.

Don's strategy seemed to work, as each pass of the plane temporarily sent the cow into the woods onshore. I decided to make a run for the calf, where camera, radio and other gear still lay, timing my arrival to match that of my cover, Don's plane. Little did I know, as I began my dash, that Don had given up the buzzing, planning instead to walk in with the rifle and rescue me. By the time I realized I was on my own, there was no turning back, so I hurriedly threw the gear into my pack and ran toward our landing area.

I never looked back, but the cow did not give chase this time. I slowed to a walk and then saw that my shirt and pants were splattered with blood, still flowing liberally from a gash on my hand. I had inadvertently cut myself as I hastily gathered up the knives, but I never felt a thing. Endorphins are powerful, indeed.

While wolves kill many calf moose, they are heavily dependent on moose older than about nine years of age, but this group comprises a small proportion of the population. Prime-age moose are too dangerous to approach; it is obviously advantageous for wolves to determine the vulnerability of a moose without getting too close. Sometimes the moose make it easy. In fact, most wolf-moose encounters end after just a few seconds, following an aggressive display by the moose.

In terms of clues that wolves might use, a running moose is a "dead giveaway." To my knowledge, no one has ever observed wolves killing a moose that did not run when first confronted by its predators. Running is often a successful escape strategy for moose, for they can easily outrun wolves in deep, soft snow. But moose commonly stand and pugnaciously face the wolves, which take the cue and leave.

In the course of its life, an individual moose evidently changes its response to wolves as it becomes older and more susceptible to attack. Moose that formerly stood their ground when wolves appeared begin to behave with less assurance, eventually resorting to a panicked run. I have observed only three limping moose in several thousand observations of moose on the ground. They are either very adept at hiding their disabilities or, more likely, are quickly culled from the population by attentive wolves.

Such vigilance, however, does not necessarily mean that wolves achieve machine-like efficiency in dispatching all moose at the first sign of weakness. For me, the most memorable proof of this occurred in 1979, when Don Murray and I investigated a black form in the middle of

Siskiwit Bay. Here we found a moose wandering in circles on the frozen surface of Lake Superior, almost a mile from the main island. When we found the moose so far from the protection of the forest, we began to circle overhead, trying to decipher the strange trail of tracks in the snow.

We followed the wanderings of the moose back to the main island and through the woods to a small opening, where we again found the circular track. On a few low passes we could see that the moose's ears were tattered and that, even though it was a bull, it had the light brown nose of a cow moose (a bull's black nose results from dark-pigmented hair generated by the male reproductive hormone, testosterone). It looked like an old, senile bull, but why the strange behavior out on Lake Superior? Don looked the ice over carefully, and decided that he could set the plane down on a smooth patch near the moose for a closer look.

Shortly thereafter, we were sliding to a stop next to the bull, which was now on its feet and stomping the ice with fury at the noisy intrusion. Don kept the engine running in case we needed to exit quickly. This was a "hand-prop" plane, and Don would have to get out and spin the propeller by hand to restart the engine.

As the moose laid back his ears and made his way toward us, we saw that each eye was a large white sphere. These were the dead eyes of a blind moose, perhaps riddled with cataracts. Our curiosity dwindled as the irritated moose continued to approach. Don gunned the engine, and we took off.

We circled back over the old blind bull and watched his head rotate as he followed our progress in the sky. Don and I fairly rubbed our hands in anticipation of what would follow, as we had just left 11 wolves of the Middle Pack bedded onshore a few miles away. If they continued their direction of travel, they should encounter this blind, senile old bull far from any protective cover.

Not wanting to miss the action, we kept checking on the moose for the remainder of the day, but it was undisturbed as the wolves slept the day away. The next morning was bright and sunny, and Don and I anxiously flew straight to Siskiwit Bay, expecting to see a maze of wolf tracks and beds around a fresh kill. There was certainly a maze of wolf tracks, but the moose was standing upright in the middle of them. We found not a drop of blood in the snow and no wounds on the moose, and we marveled at the tenacity of this old-timer. This time the mere sound of

*A blind moose, wandering in circles on
Lake Superior ice, successfully fought
off a large wolf pack.*

*The final dash for a 15-year-old cow moose that failed to
make a successful stand against the East Pack. Within two
minutes, the moose was down and the wolves were feeding.*

the plane in the sky was enough to send the moose into a tirade of stomping and kicking—he had obviously had a bad night. When the evening of the second day finally approached, the scene was unchanged— the moose was ready for all comers, and the wolves lay in silent anticipation, curled up in the same beds they were using early in the day.

Day three brought us back to the scene, this time with no certain expectations. When still five miles away, we could make out a dark spot on the ice, now a half-mile farther out on Lake Superior. "I bet they got him now!" declared Don. As we approached we gradually made out the long legs of our friend, still standing, in the middle of a new batch of wolf tracks. The wolves were gone, having decided to look elsewhere.

The next day brought a windy snowstorm, and three days passed before we were airborne again. The moose was nowhere to be found. Indeed, the ice he had been standing on was gone, taken out by the wind. We were finally left to conclude that he met his end in the big lake. This blind, old, senile bull became, in my mind, the standard by which to measure the toughness of moose when facing their age-old enemy.

*   *   *

Experience is the best teacher for a wolf learning to hunt, and the best-trained wolf I ever saw on Isle Royale was the alpha female that led the East Pack from its start in 1971 until 1981, when the entire pack vanished. She was at least 11 years old when she died. During her reign, her pack grew to 18 wolves. She outlived four mates, or alpha males, and produced 40 to 50 surviving pups.

At times in winter, her pack killed moose at a rate as high as one every 2.5 days. I conservatively estimated that, during her lifetime, this wolf killed 500 moose. I once met an old moose hunter in Sweden, a person venerated among local hunters, who had killed 400 moose—but he didn't do it with his teeth. Imagine the knowledge locked up in an old wolf after such an extraordinary life! At the standard five percent success rate, her record translates into 10,000 close encounters with moose that could have killed her with a single, well-placed kick. She undoubtedly passed along to her offspring some useful tips about "reading" a moose.

The relative inexperience of other wolves in this female's pack was revealed one winter day when she led her family of aspiring young hunters down the middle of a long lake. Ahead, we could see three moose browsing on the birch-covered lakeshore, and we circled overhead to witness the encounter. Finally, when directly across from them, the wolves saw the moose. The great hunters came to a halt and stood in line like a repeating pattern on wallpaper, heads up, ears erect, and eyes fixed on the moose.

A few seconds passed before the inexperienced rear guard broke rank and took off on a wild run, heading straight for the moose. The alpha female sat down on the ice and watched, and pilot Don Murray chuckled; they both knew nothing would come of this. The trio of moose looked out over the ice, saw the approaching bedlam, and quickly disappeared over a ridge. The neophyte wolves excitedly sniffed the tracks and the recent beds of the moose, then looked back at their mother, as if awaiting further instructions. They finally filed back onto the lake and rejoined their elders in an excited group greeting. The alpha female, indulgent of her offspring, resumed the pace.

When traveling upwind, hunting wolves usually detect moose with their noses. But researcher Roger Peters emphasized that wolves also possess what psychologists call "cognitive maps," raising the possibility that through extensive travel, wolves develop a mental catalog of individual prey. Radiocollared moose on Isle Royale become rather sedentary by midwinter, so wolves could certainly become familiar with individual moose through repeated contact. Don Murray suggested that hunting wolves search systematically for prey that they may have previously wounded. I offer the following example:

We were puzzled one morning to find the West Pack leaving its familiar shoreline travel route and heading inland after a night of unsuccessful hunting, trekking through unusually deep snow. We knew of a wounded moose on the other side of the island, fully ten miles away overland. The wolves were heading straight toward it, diagonally across the grain of the island. Three hours later they reached the wounded moose, now supported by only three good legs, and quickly dispatched it. The moose had been there, wounded and infirm, for six weeks!

*   *   *

The last photograph of the aging alpha female (top) in the East Pack, taken in 1981. She founded this pack in 1971 and led it until 1981, when the entire pack disappeared.

The last kill of the alpha female of the Middle Pack, in 1994. Standing at left, the aging female leader succumbed to old age and starvation two weeks later, teeth worn to rounded stubs. With her mate already dead, she left behind four orphaned pups which survived winter on their own.

*The alpha female of the East Pack in 1977 begins
to open up the chest cavity of a freshly killed
moose, while the alpha male rests behind her.*

*In the 1970s the East Pack developed on a portion of Isle Royale that
had not previously been given the exclusive attention of a large pack
of wolves. The pack grew eventually to be the largest on the island.*

Although they are spared from persecution by humans, Isle Royale wolves lead hard lives; the oldest wolf we know of lasted for 12 years. The wolves' teeth become too worn to be useful, and they die from starvation, accidents, or attacks by other wolves. When we are lucky enough to find the carcass of a very old wolf, it is usually easy to decipher the cause of death. Some wolves suffer complete physical deterioration; it is a wonder that they manage to stay alive as long as they do.

In 1994, the alpha pair of the Middle Pack became known to us casually as "The Old Man" and "The Old Lady." The female was graying around her muzzle and sides, and may have had other mates earlier in her life. When these two wolves paired off and claimed a territory in 1990, they were the best hope for renewed reproduction. Unfortunately their territory, dominated by mature birch in the aftermath of the 1936 burn, held very few moose. Wolf packs had not done well there since the 1970s. In August of 1991 we radiocollared the male (#550), but we found no evidence of reproduction that year. In 1992 we diligently monitored his radio signals all summer, but again we failed to locate any pups.

By 1993 there was little hope that the Middle Pack would amount to much, and we shifted our monitoring efforts to the other two packs. So when we arrived on the island in January of 1994, it was a genuine surprise to find six wolves in the Middle Pack, including four new pups! However, the alpha male's collar was in mortality mode, indicating that the wolf had not moved for four hours. We soon recovered his emaciated carcass. His teeth were severely worn, and he had simply run out of energy when the temperature bottomed out at 35° below zero.

The male had wandered away from his pack before he died, and after waiting nearby on a kill for ten days, the female led her four offspring on an extensive trek through their territory, perhaps looking for her mate. Fifty miles later, the troupe ended up back on their kill, without ever finding the male (which by then was in our freezer). We wondered about the added burden on the female of having to kill moose without much assistance.

Perhaps taking a clue from squawking ravens, she led her pack outside its territory and found a moose that had fallen to its death off a north shore cliff. It was here that we last observed the female alive, on February 7, 1994. We searched her territory in vain for a week without finding a trace of her. She was never radiocollared, so we had little hope of ever finding her body.

For three weeks, however, her four pups relaxed together on the north shore, eating a second and then a third moose that had fallen off the north shore cliffs. Both the cliff and the lake were white that winter, and the moose apparently failed to detect the drop between the two white expanses. The wolves made one quick foray back onto Middle Pack range, then returned to finish off the carcasses along the shore.

On March 1, our last flight of the 1994 winter study, we found a fresh fox track along the north shore, almost 15 miles from the pups. Looking for an excuse to stop, we landed and followed the fox tracks onshore. There, we were stunned to find the old female wolf dead, sprawled on her chest beneath a spruce tree. She had continued to travel as long as she could, and like her mate, she was emaciated with heavily worn teeth. On their one trip "home" the pups had come within a few yards of their dead mother, and they probably knew she was gone.

This alpha pair had been chronically undernourished for months, and both had lost more than a third of their body weight. Coincidentally, each wolf neared its end point after successfully raising their first litter of pups. The male, with an enlarged heart and a bruised liver, may have been pushed beyond the point of endurance by record-low temperatures. But what finally triggered the female's death a month later? Could it have been the death of her mate?

In 1894, Ernest T. Seton caught a male wolf in New Mexico that had returned to the spot where his mate had been killed a few days earlier. Seton chained the male overnight, but the wolf, despite having no apparent injury, was dead the following morning. Seton thought that distress over the death of his mate triggered the male's death. Similar incidents are well-documented in our own species.

*   *   *

One of the most interesting death scenes I have witnessed on Isle Royale involved foxes, not wolves. In February of 1973, the winter study crew sat around the picnic table, eating dinner in the kitchen of the old 1930-style barracks we inhabited. Outside, we had shoveled a narrow path leading from the door, surrounded by four-foot snowbanks on either side. Suddenly, we heard a thumping knock at the door. We paused and looked at each other, puzzled expressions on our faces. There were only four people on the island, and all were present and accounted for. Who could possibly be at the door? I was closest to the entryway, so I got up to investigate.

As I opened the door, the lights of the room revealed a fox lying on its side against the door, its mouth opening and closing rhythmically in terminal spasm. Don Murray came to the door, and together we watched the fox die—its eyes stayed open, and respiration simply stopped. I found some rubber gloves (after all, we were in the middle of a meal) and popped the fox carcass into a plastic bag, while Don went outside to investigate. When I joined him a pair of foxes, our usual backyard visitors, sat on either side of the path. Don had begun lecturing the chagrined foxes, as he often did, but his interrogation was met with innocent, wide-eyed stares. I told Don that we had to declare the audience free from guilt, as there were no tooth marks on the dead fox.

We counted the familiar faces, confirming that the fox was indeed a newcomer, a stranger to our front door. While new to the neighborhood, the fox was an old-timer with heavily worn teeth. The carcass was eventually subjected to a thorough autopsy by pathologists at Purdue University, but no obvious cause of death was determined. I could only try to imagine the social stress that must attend the arrival of a newcomer in an established group—especially one in which the social hierarchy was maintained by overt aggression. Perhaps drawn to our doorstep by desperate hunger, the old fox was suddenly beset in the dark by a crowd of unfamiliar and probably unfriendly faces. It's likely that the shock simply did him in.

Foxes tend to be high-strung, nervous creatures, and the presence of wolves certainly contributes to the daily tension of their lives on Isle Royale. The wolf's little cousins regard their larger relatives with great interest, and with a certain understandable caution. Making a living in winter by scavenging wolf kills, foxes walk a fine line between life and death. To be successful, they must learn the nuances of wolf behavior quickly, for they do not live long. Somehow, they can distinguish between an overfed wolf that is too content to move and a merely well-fed wolf that is looking for some action. I have often seen foxes cautiously approach a wolf kill and even walk among the sleeping wolves. How does a fox calculate its odds of success?

*Scavenging wolf-killed moose provides
easy bounty for foxes in winter, although
alertness near wolves is required.*

The best way for wolves to keep scavengers from a carcass is to eat it quickly, and this explains the unrestrained gluttony of wolves at a fresh kill. They are protective of their kills and show little mercy toward smaller scavengers. Dave Mech has graphically described how one wolf caught a running fox, shaking it violently: "It then carried the limp carcass under some trees. Half an hour later, I found that the wolf had ripped out the intestines of the fox and abandoned the animal, at least temporarily." I've found several foxes killed by wolves; invariably, they are full of tooth punctures and signs of a violent death, but they are uneaten.

There are exceptions to every rule, and as soon as we think we under-stand some aspect of wolf behavior, the animals surprise us. In 1990, the Middle Pack pair walked slowly one late afternoon along the icy shoreline of Todd Harbor. Suddenly the wolves broke into a vigorous run toward a small island a few hundred yards away. A red fox was the cause of the excitement, and the wolves quickly caught it, biting and tearing at both ends of the unlucky fox. A few seconds later, however, the wolves abruptly ceased their attack and walked directly off the island. After urine-marking a prominent chunk of ice, they moved on to a nearby moose kill. It was late in the breeding season, and the wolves had a full agenda. The carcass of the fox remained stretched out on the snow, just as the wolves had left it.

After following the wolves for several minutes, we returned for another close look at the fox. As we considered picking up its remains, we were astonished to see the victim sitting up. Its fur was a bit matted, but it was clearly alive and functioning. The fox slowly stood up and ambled off onto the frozen lake surface, where it sat down with its front legs spread wide, as if for added support. One rarely sees a fox sit still for long, but this one evidently had much to occupy its thoughts as it stared across the ice at the setting sun. When we returned for another look 15 minutes later, the fox had vanished.

*   *   *

Just as wolves are unwilling to share their kills with scavengers, wolf packs compete for exclusive space—their hunting grounds. We have seen ample evidence of territorial warfare between adjacent packs. In the 1980s the Harvey Lake Pack in the island's midsection was the clear underdog in such pack encounters. From 1980 to 1986 this pack led a tenuous existence, contending not only with the normal struggle to find prey and reproduce, but also with serious aggression from neighboring packs on both borders.

In 1983 we found four pups in the Harvey Lake Pack—the first definite evidence of successful reproduction within the pack. On March 1 we watched six wolves in West Pack follow tracks to a kill where the Harvey Lake Pack was feeding. The spot was situated on the ridge right behind Daisy Farm Campground, a summertime haven for boaters and backpackers. The Harvey Lake wolves ran off without hesitation as soon as the West Pack emerged at the kill site, but the West Pack alpha pair led its entire pack in a chase after the retreating wolves. The West Pack alpha wolves overtook a Harvey Lake pup, but they passed right by it—alpha wolves were their targets. Finally, after a mile-long run, the West Pack leaders caught and brought down the Harvey Lake alpha female. For about two minutes, the West Pack crowded around and attacked the alpha female, which snapped defensively and writhed on her sides and back. Then, suddenly, the pack ceased the attack and watched as the haggard female leaped up and submissively left the area.

She eventually caught up with the rest of her pack. We surmised that the alpha females of these two packs were former acquaintances, or relatives. Similarly, years later, we observed an East Pack alpha female catch and attack a lone female, then allow her to escape. These two females, radiocollared and genetically typed as sisters, had been very close earlier in their lives, before either had formed a pack or reproduced.

A year after the incident between the West Pack and the Harvey Lake Pack, we witnessed one of those surprises of animal behavior. In almost the same location, the West Pack chased down the same Harvey Lake alpha female. This time the hapless victim was killed. Another Harvey Lake female, which had been "waiting in the wings," quickly assumed the alpha female position, and the pack survived.

The East and West packs continued to persecute the Harvey Lake Pack. The final blow may have occurred on January 25, 1987. The three Harvey Lake wolves had killed a moose south of Siskiwit Lake, and they were bedded nearby with full bellies. At the other end of Siskiwit Lake, which is some seven miles long, we began watching the three-member

The East Pack attacks a loner that has ventured into pack territory in 1981. This was the final stage of harrassment, and the alpha female (tail raised, far left) is already departing the scene.

The triple calling card of an alpha wolf—a fresh scat, scratch marks, and a vigorous, raised-leg urination directed at a stump.

Almost clone-like in outward appearance, these two pups trailed their parents in the West Pack in 1988. These were the last pups to appear in the island's western half through 1995.

East Pack as they traveled on a collision course over the ice of the frozen lake. The East Pack moved confidently, their tracks an unwavering line. They soon encountered the trail of the Harvey Lake Pack, and we circled overhead as major decisions were made. The East Pack alpha male took the lead, but he often stopped to wait for the alpha female, which greeted him as they excitedly rubbed sides and resumed the quest.

As the East Pack left the lake on a trail leading to the kill, they began exploring the maze of trails left by the Harvey Lake wolves. During one portion of our circle through the air, we saw the contented Harvey Lake wolves, the alpha pair bedded and the third wolf feeding. While banking on the other side of our circle, we watched mayhem closing in. When they were 100 yards from the kill, the East Pack wolves suddenly halted and stared briefly ahead; they then plunged through untracked snow, heading directly for the Harvey Lake alpha pair. The bedded wolves rose quickly and took off in different directions, but the alpha male was the slowest. The East Pack wolves quickly singled him out. They rapidly gained ground on the alpha male, pulling him down on his back within 200 yards.

The Harvey Lake alpha male snapped defensively and shoved vigorously with all four feet as three wolves bit and tore at him. The East Pack alpha pair attacked only his neck and chest, while the third wolf worked on his posterior. The attackers shook their heads violently after tightly clamping their teeth onto their victim. About five minutes after initial contact, blood appeared in the snow beneath the alpha male's head. However, after 12 minutes of the battle, the victim managed to leap to his feet briefly before he was slammed back down. The attack then resumed as before, and the white teeth of the Harvey Lake alpha male continued to flash in vigorous defense. The wolf made two more heroic efforts to rise, but after 20 minutes he was unable to raise his head. His legs continued kicking, but these movements gradually slowed and finally ceased. After moving away and lying down for a few moments, the East Pack renewed the attack, biting, shaking, and dragging the downed wolf.

At the 30-minute mark, the three wolves halted their attack and walked away from the motionless carcass. When we later landed to recover the victim, we found that the wolf had died of massive internal injuries. The dead wolf weighed 94 pounds. If it were not for 12 pounds of moose packed into his stomach, he might have escaped! In subsequent years we saw no further sign of the Harvey Lake Pack; in fact, no reproducing pack would appear in the middle of the island for another seven years.

Wolves may disappear mysteriously, leaving even their own associates to wonder what happened. Male #470 and female #670 were close partners for over two years, headquartered at the west end of Isle Royale even though they didn't claim a territory of their own with scent marks. Although they never reproduced, we considered them a mated pair. They often separated, especially in summer, but they were a consistent couple each winter from 1989 through 1991. Yet in February of 1991, female #670 abruptly departed from her usual range and her male friend, heading for the other end of Isle Royale.

One night, before she reached the far end of the island, her radio signal suddenly disappeared. The next morning we found no tracks that might have been hers, so we turned to male #470 in the hope that he could find her. Indeed, he seemed to take up the task. A few days after she abandoned him, he traveled 40 miles to the northeast, killed a moose, then remained alone near the kill for several days. He then abruptly returned to the west end and curled up on the pinnacle of a small island, near a travel route he had often used with female #670. He spent two days looking over the harbor, and we presumed he was waiting for his mate to reappear. But she never returned, and male #470 then moved back to the island's northeast end. He quickly located female #590, a wolf he had courted two years before. By then it was early March, the end of the breeding season, but perhaps it was not too late to reproduce. We were forced to close the book on female #670, and her presumed death became one of those nagging uncertainties instead of an event that could teach us something.

Over two years later, in May of 1993, a beachcomber near Malone Bay happened on the remains of a wolf, freshly washed up on shore. The head was still covered with hair and flesh, but the rest of the body was a skin-covered skeleton. A fox had pulled a radio collar from the wolf onto the rocks and then abandoned it, and the bright morning light revealed the numerals "670" on the inside of the collar. We received word of the discovery and gladly accepted the bag turned in by the hiker, which contained the rotting wolf's head and radiocollar.

So the old saying that Lake Superior never gives up her dead is not completely true—but she certainly deliberates long and hard before doing

Yearling female #1071 was killed while trespassing, after taking up with a young male from the adjacent East Pack. The male's mother, female #450, probably led the attack—she was tending the carcass of #1071 a day later, then she died herself.

so! The wolf evidently went through thin ice in an unfamiliar bay of Lake Superior, then died and sank to a depth where decomposition was very slow and her radio signal was buried. After being carried underwater for at least 16 miles by the prevailing currents, she surfaced. With extraordinary luck, we reopened and finally completed a unique case history among our "research wolves." We can only presume that male #470 never did figure out the fate of his former mate.

Radio collars have enabled us to learn that certain individuals can determine the direction and fate of the larger wolf population and indirectly influence the ecology of the entire island. Each year during the 1990s, we carefully scrutinized the East Pack for female #450, a wolf that outlasted the batteries in her radio collar. She became progressively whiter with age, and by 1993 we expected her demise at any time. As a middle-aged female in 1988, she had been the first wolf live-captured and radiocollared on Isle Royale. She had never reproduced, and she associated loosely with two other wolves. This group made a living, but they had no

Female #450 was the first Isle Royale wolf to be live-captured and radiocollared.
The ten pups she bore between 1991 and 1994 comprised most of the next
generation of wolves and saved the population from extinction.

exclusive territory and they gave little indication of future success. In 1989, female #450 left this little group forever and moved into the East Pack, where her sister was an alpha female. Somehow, female #450 acquired her sister's pups and became the alpha female; her sister was banished from the pack.

The outcast wolf lived another 18 months within her old territory, often following the East Pack and watching them from a safe distance. She presented a poignant sight the next winter as she lay on a cliff edge, watching her pups, her sister, and her former mate dine below on a fresh kill. The best she could hope for was to scavenge a few frozen bones after the pack left.

Although an unchallenged leader in the East Pack, female #450 did not have pups of her own until 1991. Her ten surviving pups between

1991 and 1994 helped stay the threat of wolf extinction. In January of 1995, we were honestly surprised to find her still alive at 11 to 15 years of age. She seemed in poor condition—she was gaunt, with skin draped over the outline of her skeleton. I expected that her death was imminent, and I hoped to learn about her final chapter.

During her last month of life, she continued to lead her pack of six wolves. She sat out some of the extravagant chases, as when the alpha male and the younger members of the pack took off over the ice after a passing fox. Many of her offspring had dispersed from their home pack during the previous year, but early in 1995 one of her sons returned to his natal territory, accompanied by a radiocollared female from the adjacent Middle Pack. This pair killed a moose in East Pack territory, and their playful courtship lent an optimistic cast to the future. This was exactly the kind of pairing we had hoped for in wolves of the next generation, when we might learn the implications of genetic decay unfettered by low food supply or disease.

On January 30, 1995, female #450 and her pack discovered a moose recently killed by this pair. The next day (while we were grounded by poor weather), the East Pack caught the pair several miles from the kill, then killed the Middle Pack female in a violent struggle. Twenty-four hours later, when we became aware of the event and arrived on the scene, only female #450 remained at the carcass of the dead female. The old alpha female was carefully eating flesh from the dead wolf's rib cage; the internal organs had already been consumed, presumably by ravens and wolves. Never before had I seen a wolf eat another, even after killing it. She had emerged the victor in this battle for dominance. Obviously, old female #450 had more spunk than I had believed possible.

We landed on a nearby lake and snowshoed to retrieve the dead wolf. As we emerged at the site, a live wolf disappeared into the shadows of the nearby forest. Surrounding the dead wolf was an awesome spectacle, and we pieced together from tracks how the hapless female had been chased off a low cliff, caught below by the East Pack, and died after a protracted struggle that left 30 yards of bloody snow and broken branches. The young female had lasted a long time; her attackers never succeeded in inflicting any mortal wounds around her vulnerable neck or head, and she had cracked off two premolar teeth in her final effort.

We never saw female #450 again. Killing her rival from the Middle Pack was her last act, and it evidently claimed her final reserve of energy. In the next month we searched diligently for her, by air and on the ground, but we never found a clue. For us, another mystery; we will search for her bones and her worn radio collar under trees and rocks for many years to come. She was quickly replaced in the pack hierarchy by a daughter, and the life of the East Pack resumed.

The alpha male in the East Pack was left with only a couple of pups and two of his own adult daughters in the pack, so mating and reproduction were uncertain in 1995. "Murder, cannibalism, and incest," muttered a colleague, shaking his head at the conduct of the wolves. Henry Beston's words came to my mind: "We need another and wiser and perhaps more mystical concept of animals . . . For the animal shall not be measured by man . . . They are not brethren, they are not underlings; they are other nations, caught in . . . the splendour and travail of the earth."

Questions of immortality probably do not interest wolves. But their quest to survive, reproduce, and secure resources so that their offspring can carry on with life is unmistakably powerful. The legacy of female #450 was much greater than that left behind by the "average" wolf. Her late-blooming reproduction, modest though it was, allowed the dramatic experiment of wolf survival to continue on Isle Royale into the late 1990s. Though she would care not a whit, science owes something to this old wolf, and to her, in a detached way, I am most grateful.

Fenced in by Lake Superior, wildlife populations on Isle Royale are unable to move in and out of the study area, making annual counts more meaningful to scientists.

Life in a Microcosm

. . . in (our) brain there is really only a sort of universal marsh, spotted at intervals by quaking green islands representing the elusive stability of modern science— islands frequently gone as soon as glimpsed.
        Loren Eiseley, *The Firmament of Time,* 1960

SINCE AT LEAST THE DAYS OF DARWIN, ISLANDS HAVE been wonderful places for the exercise of biology. When islands support a reduced number and unique combination of species, they can facilitate extraordinary experiments in ecology and evolution. The scientific value of an island depends both on what is there and what is not there. At Isle Royale, the dominant players for the last half-century have been a single predator species and its prey; the element missing was hunting by humans.

Among most warm-blooded animals, the larger an animal is, the longer its life, the slower its pace of living, and the longer its generations. One of the greatest challenges in ecology is to understand phenomena that occur slowly; humans are an impatient, inattentive species and want quick answers. After decades of study on Isle Royale, it is safe to say that we are still low on the learning curve, and each new discovery may change the way we explain the past. Predicting the future, an activity humans seem unable to resist, is impossible. Perhaps that is the greatest lesson of all.

The essential ecological questions for wolf and moose research at Isle Royale have always been "*How* do their populations change over time?" and "*Why* do they fluctuate as they do?" In the past 35 years, two generations of scientists have been well-occupied studying several generations of moose and perhaps a half-dozen turnovers of wolves. Even this "simple" system has proven marvelously complicated.

In the late 1950s, when studies of wolves and moose were begun on Isle Royale, there were few wolves left in the United States following three centuries in which humans had devised ingenious and highly efficient methods of killing them. The application of science to discovering the nature of wolf predation was limited to the pioneering work of Adolph Murie in Mt. McKinley (now Denali) National Park, published in 1944, and early investigations in Minnesota, conducted by Sigurd F. Olson in the 1930s and Milt Stenlund in the 1950s. When Durward Allen sent graduate student Dave Mech to Isle Royale in 1958, Alaska had just become a state, and a decade of federal wolf control by poisoning and aerial gunning ended as the state assumed jurisdiction over resident wildlife. A few hundred wolves could still be found in northeastern Minnesota, but they had a bounty on their heads. Elsewhere in America (though not in Canada) the wolf had been eliminated. Humans had presumed themselves ecological engineers, with no idea how the machinery of nature worked. Isle Royale became the perfect place to find out.

Many techniques of animal study were unknown or in experimental stages during the 1950s. The first aircraft counts of moose anywhere in the world were performed at Isle Royale, just after the end of World War II. A decade later, federal agents in Alaska started using light aircraft to study wolves rather than to shoot them. Revelations were forthcoming—not the least of which was the realization that a single pack of wolves covered a gigantic area.

An important early question for Mech involved testing Murie's assertion that wolves seemed to cull the old, the infirm, and the very young from their prey. In three years, after locating wolf-killed moose from aircraft in winter and moose skeletons on the ground in summer, Mech had a sample of 107 moose that had died on the island. Even though the relative age of moose could be estimated only by toothwear, the conclusion at Isle Royale was very clear—wolves did not kill moose at random.

Determining the age of a wild animal is essential for any understanding of its population growth and decline. In the 1950s, as a first improvement over simple guesswork, Randolph Peterson in Ontario described nine more or less discrete classes of toothwear for moose. However, no one knew how many years moose actually lived.

Mech's direct observations of hunting wolves showed that most moose were "tested" by wolves, then abandoned as too dangerous. Calf moose were clearly at risk, and together with old adults, comprised most wolf kills. Using the nine classes of toothwear for moose and excluding calves, Mech found that 29 of 32 wolf-killed moose he examined in winter belonged in the last three of the nine classes of toothwear. Examining and collecting bones from as many dead moose as possible became a long-term scientific tradition at Isle Royale.

A decade later, Michael Wolfe applied a new technique of age determination to the collection of Isle Royale moose jaws, counting cementum annulations (visible indicators rather like tree rings) in cross-sections of teeth. He found that moose lived as long as 20 years, and he derived an average schedule for mortality in relation to age—an actuarial table for moose. Isle Royale still provides the best information available on patterns of natural mortality for moose in the absence of the gun. Ironically, one of the most important applications of such knowledge lies in the management of moose hunting elsewhere, in order to align the effects of hunting by humans as closely as possible with the age-old pattern wrought by predation.

*   *   *

Regarding many wildlife populations, the first question asked and often the most difficult to answer is, "How many animals are there?" The ups and downs of animal populations are both practically and theoretically important. Stability in the wolf population was immediately evident in Mech's initial work at Isle Royale, as 20, 22, and 20 wolves were counted in each of the first three years. No wolf dens or other evidence of reproduction were found, so low reproduction and turnover were evidently part of the story.

Counting moose accurately has always been a difficult challenge, as

*The author examines
an annual collection
of moose bones.*

*Scavengers both, pilot Don Glaser
and a fox wrestle with the spoils
at a wolf kill.*

moose tend to spend a lot of time in winter beneath spruce and fir trees, where they may be totally obscured from observers in aircraft. In 1960 Mech attempted a complete count of moose by flying overlapping strips and found 512 animals. Allowing for those missed, he estimated that 600 moose were present. His mapped distribution of moose showed heavy concentrations in the 1936 burn area, and in a much smaller 1948 burn. This was virtually the last time such a pattern was observed.

Mech's estimates of the number of moose that were born and the number that died each year were nearly equal (83 and 85 respectively), and his inference of a stable prey population was reasonable. Furthermore, moose showed little evidence of nutritional limitation. Indeed, their twinning rates (the frequency at which twin calves are born), a reflection of nutritional well-being, were among the highest on record for moose. In his Ph.D. thesis, published in 1966 as part of the Park Service Fauna Series, Mech reported that wolves had stabilized moose within the limits of their food supply. For the next two decades, biology and ecology textbooks reported that wolves had brought stability to Isle Royale.

Through the 1960s Durward Allen continued the winter monitoring of wolves and moose, and graduate student Dave Mech was followed by Philip Shelton, Peter Jordan, and Michael Wolfe. For an entire decade, the wolf population remained remarkably stable, hovering between 20 and 28 individuals. In the mid-1960s Peter found evidence of wolf reproduction, in the form of a den dug out in March and a pup that had starved to death on the shore of an interior lake.

However, even though the population remained about the same each year, wolf pack structure changed markedly. Canadian biologist Douglas Pimlott hypothesized in a 1967 article that wolves were limited by social behavior to a maximum density of one per ten square miles, largely inferred from the 20 or so wolves typically found on Isle Royale's 210 square miles. It was thought unlikely that wolves would ever become more numerous.

As the 1960s progressed, new techniques were used to assess the moose population. At Isle Royale and elsewhere, strip counts of moose in winter were found unsatisfactory. Instead, a network of small plots was established, to be intensively counted from circling aircraft. The new estimates of moose numbers were often higher than Mech's count of 600, but the margins of error were too large to refute the original figure. The idea of a stable equilibrium at Isle Royale became ingrained.

Each winter there was another aerial count of moose to interpret. By 1970, only a couple of things were consistent about these counts—population estimates were almost always higher than Mech's 1960 figure, and the estimates were highly variable. Mike Wolfe's estimate of 1,360 moose in 1969 was the highest number attained, and he felt it was the most reliable census of the late 1960s. If this was true, then either Mech's 1960 count was too low or the population had increased significantly. A moose increase was also suggested by periodic counts of winter moose droppings by biologist Laurits Krefting. Slowly accumulating evidence eventually confirmed that the moose population had been on the rise.

If wolves had not stabilized the moose, then perhaps moose were *not* being maintained within the limits of their food supply, as Mech had postulated. Perhaps the notion of a stable equilibrium was incorrect, and the famous balance between wolves and moose, widely cited and recited in literature and classrooms, might be a gross oversimplification. In 1970, when I began my own graduate work, the issue of moose population stability was a most pertinent one, but inherent technical problems remained that could mask real population changes.

Someone once pointed out that understanding population regulation in a stable population was analogous to trying to discern the properties of gravity by watching an apple hanging motionless in a tree. To see the whole picture at Isle Royale requires a long-term and wide-angle perspective. Dramatic events greeted us in the early 1970s, and conclusions based solely on these years would have been far different from those of the previous decade. In three of the four winters between 1969 and 1972, snow depths exceeded 30 inches—the belly height of moose calves—and wolves simply mowed them down in winter. Bone measurements confirmed that many of these calves were nutritionally deprived "runts," born after winters of deep snow. As the moose population declined, longtime visitors to Isle Royale began to see the changes, and frequently asked what had happened to all the moose.

When writing my Ph.D. dissertation in 1974, I reported that moose had not been kept within the limits of their food supply, and that the wolf population had increased. Venturing out on the thin ice of limited understanding, I asserted that these changes were due to moose habitat, with weather serving as an important factor in limiting browse for moose. Second growth aspen and birch forests within the 1936 and 1948 burn areas had grown up and were no longer satisfactory winter habitat for moose. These were the areas that supported most of the moose observed by Mech in 1960.

Moose were now forced to exist in older forests, where there was less to eat. Their food supply had contracted, I thought, and the moose population was brought into alignment in the early 1970s by an impressive increase in wolf predation. Nature's balance, adjusted but still neat and tidy, seemed confirmed, albeit with a few new twists. The implication was that habitat functioned as the ultimate regulator of moose density on Isle Royale, and that wolf predation was simply the executor of nature's will.

Dave Mech and I agreed in 1976 that, while some details remained to be fleshed out, the major "hows" and "whys" of moose-wolf dynamics at Isle Royale seemed to be pretty well wrapped up. At that point, Dave urged me to consider doing another study of moose and wolves—this time in Alaska. Not willing to pass up such an extraordinary opportunity, I was nonetheless unwilling to call it quits at Isle Royale. So I did both. For a few years, the wolves of the Kenai Peninsula in Alaska were a major diversion. Isle Royale was temporarily on the back burner of my schedule, with only a single stint of field work scheduled for me there each winter. Nature proceeded in my absence, however, and eventually forced me to revisit my earlier conclusions.

By the late 1970s winter weather had moderated, but wolves continued to increase, and the moose population continued to decline. Summertime moose sightings by park visitors became almost embarrassingly infrequent. If wolf predation was simply fine-tuning moose numbers to fit the habitat, then we must not understand moose habitat very well. Wolves continued to hammer the moose, and the wolf population, seemingly crowded with three packs, added a fourth and even a fifth pack. Lined up almost within sight of each other were packs numbering up to 18 wolves. Their combined kill rate exceeded one moose per day in winter, and their annual kill in winter alone exceeded one-fifth of the moose population. Under such phenomenal pressure, something had to give.

In 1979 I received a letter from the noted naturalist Sigurd F. Olson,

Moose calves conserve energy by following their mothers through deep snow. When threatened by wolves, however, a cow moose instinctively moves to protect the vulnerable rear of her calf, leaving the calf to break trail.

During the annual moose count in February, we prepare the research aircraft for flight before dawn, as the moon is setting.

*In winter, when bull moose are antlerless,
direct antagonism is rare. The foraging paths
of these bulls were simply too close together.*

who had studied wolves in Minnesota during the 1930s and had gone on
to a distinguished career in conservation. As a youth, I had thoroughly
absorbed Sig's books on wilderness, and this author occupied a prominent
spot in my private pantheon of respected elders. In his carefully written
letter, Sig Olson wondered if things weren't getting a bit out of hand at
Isle Royale, and he suggested that "something" might have to be done.
This was a bit reminiscent of a little-known recommendation forwarded
by Adolph Murie after he returned to Mt. McKinley National Park
following World War II and found the Dall sheep population severely
reduced. Causes for the sheep decline were unknown, but as a precaution-
ary measure he suggested that wolves should be killed inside the park to
help the sheep recover. This was actually done at McKinley in the late
1940s, but in 1979 such a move at Isle Royale was unthinkable. Isle Royale
was the only national park in America where we had allowed wolves
unrestricted life. I quietly filed Sig's letter away, pleased that he was paying
attention.

By 1980 the wolf population numbered 50—the highest year-round
wolf density ever documented in nature. One year later, we found only 30
wolves; and in the following year, just 14 remained. Newton's apple had

not just fallen from the tree, it had left an impact crater on the ground! Abruptly, the golden years for Isle Royale wolves had sputtered and died, and I struggled to find an explanation that would describe the whole picture at Isle Royale.

*　　*　　*

Even after years of heavy predation, Isle Royale's moose population persisted at a relatively high density. Could the dramatic population swings in moose and wolves have anything to do with moose habitat, confirming my original conclusion? Perhaps a fresh start was necessary in order for real scientific progress so, together with graduate students Richard Page and Kenneth Risenhoover, I once again asked a basic question: "Why does Isle Royale have so many moose?" While mainland areas in North America may have one moose or less than one per square mile, over several decades Isle Royale moose have often existed at densities greater than *five* per square mile.

The classical explanation for elevated populations on islands is referred to by ecologists as the "fence effect," where animals normally siphoned off by dispersal to other areas are retained in the population. Yet in Scandinavia, moose density is comparable to that found on Isle Royale; something other than a fence effect must explain high moose numbers.

Could it be that Isle Royale simply provides more food, or better habitat, for moose than any other locale in North America? In the time-tested notion of an ecological hierarchy, in which plants support the herbivores and herbivores in turn support the carnivores, a "bottom-up" infusion of more plants should lead to more of everything else. Indeed, during the growing season, Isle Royale looks positively tropical compared to the stunted forests growing on permafrost in interior Alaska, where trees resemble pipe cleaners or, at best, bottlebrushes. Yet the sparse birch and pine forests of Scandinavia grow just as slowly as those in Alaska, but somehow much higher moose densities are attained in Scandinavia.

What does Isle Royale have in common with Scandinavia that might indicate how the moose become so numerous? Remarkably, each year more moose are shot by hunters in Sweden than are shot in all of North America! In Scandinavia, where only a small, remnant brown bear population and a fledgling stock of wolves remain, humans are the only predators of any consequence for local moose populations. Around the world, wherever high-density moose populations exist, no more than one major predator species is present.

Isle Royale's wolves are the only predator of consequence for the island's moose. Scandinavia has plenty of experienced sharpshooters, but few wild carnivores. It is difficult to find a place where bears prey on moose in the absence of wolves and humans, but Gaspesie Provincial Park in Quebec, a place noted for its moose-viewing opportunities, appears to qualify. Could it be that the world of moose is really top-down, not bottom-up? Could it be that predators really call the shots, and that habitat is a secondary consideration? This is an important question for conservation of large carnivores, as it recognizes intense competition among predatory species. As an example of this sort of competition, humans have certainly been intolerant toward any species with sharp canine teeth. Modern human societies the world over are reluctant to allow bears and wolves to take a very large helping, even in a place like Yellowstone. Isle Royale's balance thus depends both on wolves, which cull the very young, old, and infirm moose, and on humans, who allow the system to function without interference.

While lack of predation seems to explain high moose density, what causes the dramatic fluctuations in moose numbers? We pursued this question with renewed vigor in the 1980s, and we were armed with a few refinements of our approach to moose counting. One such "improvement" was the miserable addition of a pre-dawn takeoff, which required finding the plane with a flashlight in temperatures as low as -30°F, then warming the engine block with a propane heater for half an hour in order to be in the air over our first census plot at first light. Moose are more reliably seen from aircraft at sunrise as they move about to feed.

Actually, our most effective new moose counting technique came not from the cockpit of an aircraft, but from the steel shelves where, since 1958, the bones of Isle Royale moose had been accumulating under the scrutiny of various university administrators. Because our technique of searching for kills in the winter and skeletons in the summer had been so consistent, the number of moose we recovered after death was a constant proportion of those alive in the population. Dead moose, then, were used

The cold expanse of Lake Superior has prevented most
of the mammals from the mainland from reaching
Isle Royale, resulting in a simplified ecosystem.

to "reconstruct" the population and its age structure at the time those same moose had been alive. There is a long lag in getting this information, as a generation of moose has to pass completely before we can say how many were present. Still, population reconstruction provides the best indication of historical changes in the size and age structure of the Isle Royale moose population.

In simple mathematical models of population dynamics, cycles can be induced by introducing a time lag—such as a delayed increase in predators following an increase in their prey. A striking feature of wolf and moose fluctuations at Isle Royale was the very long lag—about ten years—between successive peaks in moose and wolf numbers. Yet from 1959 to 1980 we found a close correspondence, on a year by year basis, between the number of wolves on the island and the number of moose between 10 and 20 years old. Old moose were the wolves' bread and butter, comprising about 85 percent of the actual food intake for wolves in winter. If there were plenty of old moose, the number of wolves could increase. But more wolves meant that fewer moose calves would survive their critical first year. After several years of high wolf numbers, there would be a relative scarcity of young moose in the population, and wolves would feel the shortage of vulnerable moose a decade later. Oversimplified, this is how a wolf-moose cycle might work in a strictly top-down world.

* * *

The many years of heavy predation on moose in the 1970s exerted a telling influence on the forest of Isle Royale, allowing trees to grow and, in some cases, to escape the reach of feeding moose. In the early 1980s the moose themselves were in great physical shape, and we could thank the wolves for this phenomenon. When wolves declined and young calf moose finally had a chance to capitalize on the new forest growth, they grew into such handsome yearlings that I had to keep reminding myself I was look-ing at an Isle Royale moose, not a giant from the mountains of Alaska.

The essential role of the wolf in the transformation of the forest and the rejuvenation of moose cannot be overemphasized. Finally, in the 1980s at Isle Royale, the old story that wolves protect a forest from an over-abundance of feasting herbivores was borne out. Nowhere in evidence was the habitat decline I had anticipated; nor had moose populations diminished. As soon as the weight of wolf predation was lifted in the early 1980s, calf abundance increased threefold, and it was obvious that the moose population was heading upward again. It seemed that history was about to repeat itself, and that we were observing a cycle between a great predator and its prey. Populations of much smaller mammals tend to cycle at regular intervals—three to four years for voles, and ten years for snowshoe hares, for example. Demographic cycles in moose, with a much longer generation time, must be on the order of two to three decades.

There are many influences, small and large, living and non-living, that can perturb a pattern. A tough winter, a dry summer, or a disease organism may deliver a shock to a predator-prey system, as when ticks harass moose for a year or two, or when wolves die in a bout of distemper or parvovirus. Large-scale abiotic slams, such as forest destruction by fire or storm-driven winds, may set an ecosystem on end for decades, reversing the chain of command through bottom-up control and releasing the carnivores' grip.

A major improvement in habitat on a large scale, as in the new forest growth that follows wildfire, may reinvigorate a moose population and permit it to escape the bounds of predation for a long time. Moose increased dramatically on Alaska's Kenai Peninsula after large fires in 1947 and 1969. Human hunters and bears (black bears and grizzlies) coexisted with moose in 1947, and by 1969 wolves also had recovered in the area. The number of moose living in the newly productive habitat increased, despite all predatory obstacles.

Conversely, a series of years with high snow accumulations can devastate moose populations by imprisoning them in snow for many weeks during the period when cow moose are pregnant. Historic declines of moose in Alaska have been correlated with severe winters, during which 50 percent of a moose population may perish. At Isle Royale such events have been rare, and 35 years of study is a laughably small stretch of time in which to evaluate the effect of severe winter weather that might occur only a few times in a century. Weather records from nearby Thunder Bay during the 1950s reveal two stretches of four consecutive winters with annual snowfall exceeding anything we have observed since 1958, the inception of wolf-moose research at Isle Royale. In 1960 the moose

Balsam fir provides most of the winter diet for moose on Isle Royale. At the northeast end of the island, fir grows at high density and escapes suppression by feeding moose (top). At the southwestern end, fir is less common, and with few exceptions, regeneration of this tree species is absent (bottom).

Superlative antlers on a yearling bull signify a healthy
moose born in the early 1980s, after years of low
moose density made improved nutrition available.

In winter a moose spends 12 out of every 24 hours eating
while on the move, and the remaining time is spent
bedded and ruminating, or "chewing its cud."

population was estimated, by both direct count and later reconstruction from collections of dead moose, at only 600 animals, lower than it has been at any time since then. It seems inconceivable that a few newly arrived wolves could have had much to do with this, when moose were allegedly dying off from malnutrition only a decade before. Observers at Yellowstone before 1988 did not know the scale of natural wildfire, and today at Isle Royale we have to admit that we still do not fully appreciate the power of snow.

Tiny organisms can bring megafauna to their knees, sometimes with long-lasting effects. The aftershocks of the introduction of canine parvovirus to Isle Royale continued 15 years later, when survival of the wolf population was still in question. And the diminutive winter tick, when aggregated by the tens of thousands on an individual, may kill more moose in a winter than all the large carnivores combined. We do not know exactly what causes a heavy tick year such as 1989. Springtime weather, the essence of unpredictability, seems to play a major role.

Creeping in through my mind's back door in the 1980s, as shock followed shock, was the possibility that any single equilibrium, even a dynamic equilibrium, might be a myth. The addition of major discontinuities to what might otherwise be a smooth wolf-moose cycle makes for a less predictable world—what ecologist Dan Botkin calls a "discordant harmony," which is quite unlike the symphony expected in an equilibrium. For a few measures all the instruments might seem to play a single theme, but as the concert proceeds, listeners begin to realize that each player is following a different score. The longer we listen, the less able the audience will be to predict the overall direction of the piece.

For ecologists, the spectre of a "disequilibrium system," in which the subjects are jarred unpredictably back and forth by a welter of influences, is disconcerting. Large, long-lived species such as wolves and moose can withstand many of life's vicissitudes, warding off starvation, extreme weather, shortages of prey, or surplus predators, but sooner or later a rare combination of events will turn the tide. The longer we observe a system like Isle Royale, the more shocks we see; as variability increases, our interpretations become more circumspect, more cautious, more tentative.

This is not a sign of growing incompetence or scientific senility. It actually illustrates a classical paradox in science, wherein the longer one studies a particular living system, the less one can say with certainty about its behavior. We may show improvement in our ability to explain what has just happened, but we must ever be humble in predicting what lies immediately ahead. This is the essence of a world of "disequilibrium." Even in true chaos, if one can stand far enough away, patterns may be discerned, but they are unlikely to resemble the simple notions of an earlier day. Linus Pauling, a scientist whom many rank in the company of Newton, Darwin, and Einstein, said in an interview just before his death at the age of 93, "I don't care to comment about the future of anything."

While shocks to the wolf-moose system in the 1980s were a disquieting challenge to conventional thinking, they also provided unprecedented opportunities to learn about the pervasive significance of wolves on Isle Royale. Ironically, in what seems to be the world's most secure sanctuary for wolves, disease may have resulted in one of the most effective wolf control programs of the last 20 years. The corresponding increase in moose, catapulting them to a level not seen for 60 years, showed that wolf predation had been the major force keeping moose in check during the 1960s and 1970s. And regrowth of the forest had been permitted by the high wolf and low moose numbers of the 1970s. Tree ring studies in the 1990s showed that woody vegetation was suppressed by the increasing moose population, and that the growth rates of balsam fir in the forest understory cycled in synchrony with the wolf population. When wolf numbers were high, the forest grew. What an impressive achievement for a couple of dozen wolves that were just doing what comes naturally!

In another two or three decades, if we are fortunate, we will probably look back at the 1990s and smile at the shallowness of our current understanding. That will be the best indication that we have taken proper advantage of the natural laboratory provided by Isle Royale.

*The isolated wilderness of Isle Royale heals from 19th century wounds and functions with*out *direction from humans for the past half century. The wolf decline of the 1980s and 1990s may force us to consider whether we should determine which species will inhabit the island.*

Promises to Keep

*'Natural' is a magician's word—and like all such entities,
it should be used sparingly lest there arise from it, as now,
some unglimpsed, unintended world, some monstrous
caricature called into being by the indiscreet articulation
of worn syllables.*

Loren Eiseley, *The Firmament of Time,* 1960

THE SUN SHONE AUSPICIOUSLY ON A BRIGHT APRIL
morning in 1988. I felt inappropriately bundled up in
the warmest clothes I owned as our 26-foot National
Park Service patrol boat nudged its way through a vast
field of half-inch-thick ice in the middle of Lake Superior. I heard a sound like the tinkling of fragmented glass
as broken shards of ice skittered across the frozen
surface on both sides of the boat. But the "night ice"
would be gone by midday, shattered by the slighest of
breezes across the world's largest expanse of fresh water.

The fine weather was a good omen, yet our mission
and our boatload of wolf traps engendered a sense of
foreboding. For the first time, the wolves of Isle Royale
were to become targets, and I, their longtime observer
and admirer, would become "the hunter." In my heart,
I didn't much care for the idea of capturing them—
even for purposes of temporary study. But I felt
compelled to expose them to possible risks, in order to
ascertain the causes of their decline and possible
extinction.

For years many people maintained that an aura

surrounded the Isle Royale wolves, simply because they had never been handled by humans. We had considered leaving the wolves untouched, allowing them to live or die without an attempt on our part to understand why, but scientists and managers both inside and outside the National Park Service rejected this option. After thirty-odd years of observation, it was important to write the next, and perhaps the last, chapter with the best possible knowledge. Yet for the wolves and for me, nothing would ever again be quite the same.

I wondered if any of the 12 wolves remaining on Isle Royale were watching the approach of our boat, with its synchronous drone of twin engines and its smell of gasoline. The old animals among them surely knew that people and machines routinely appear in spring, and that wolves would once again have to yield the island's network of hiking trails. But surely no wolf could anticipate my plans to capture and examine them, and this thought bothered me. For almost 20 years, I had accorded them every privilege of complete freedom. My behavior, on behalf of science, had always been benign and predictable, and perhaps they had learned to trust me.

Time for reflection ended when the patrol boat dumped park staffer Bob Krumenaker and me on the rocky beach at our summer research cabin, along with a veritable mountain of gear. It was too late to change our minds.

Bob was the natural resource management specialist for Isle Royale National Park, and he and I together had borne much of the burden of response to the "wolf crisis" of the late 1980s. Now, for a few precious days, we were the only people on the big island—all 210 square miles of it. We allowed ourselves one day to walk the trails and choose a few short miles along which to set up our trapline. We enthused over each bit of fresh wolf sign, glad to find that there were still some wolves left and thankful that they were traveling the very trails we planned to trap.

Along the barren stretches and during lunch, Bob and I had the opportunity to chat. Over the previous six months, we had been consumed by all the details of our immediate task. Now we quickly dispensed with our mental checklists of procedures and wolf-trapping paraphernalia, which we had gone over countless times before, and went on to tackle larger matters. On a bright day in spring, it seems that one can solve all problems of the world.

Bob and I agreed that it was wise to take the risk involved in handling the wolves, but we found ourselves on opposite sides when we addressed the question, "What should we do if all the wolves on Isle Royale die out?" For me, it was a disquieting discussion, for I then realized that NPS managers might allow wolves on Isle Royale to disappear, and might not welcome wolves back unless they returned of their own accord. The wolf-prey system that had worked so well for so long might simply end—period.

There is no land management agency in the United States that more earnestly seeks to preserve nature than the National Park Service. In recent decades, the Service has moved strongly toward nonintervention as a primary strategy, especially in large parks free of crushing outside influences. Bob Krumenaker was often more willing to consider alternatives than the agency he worked for, but in this case Bob was an able spokesman for the view that the wildness of Isle Royale would be diminished if, for any reason, humans tried to reverse wolf extinction on the island. We both agreed that these wolves played a vital role in a wild community. For me, the operative word was "vital," while Bob dwelt on "wild." According to Park Service management philosophy in the late 20th century, the *wild* portion of *wilderness* depends on minimizing overt human manipulation.

One person cannot hope to present objectively all the legitimate views on what the Park Service should do in the event of imminent wolf extinction on Isle Royale. Bob and I took a stab at this in a paper published in 1989[1], but the questions we raised were too hypothetical (or distressing) to be taken very seriously then. At that time, we introduced most of the issues I again address here.

With the benefit of more knowledge and further exploration of Park Service policies, this chapter represents my own perspective on future options for wolves on Isle Royale. To the extent that I can, I've tried to enunciate all possible viewpoints, in the hope that the National Park Service—and the public—will pay attention. This exploration of management possibilities was my own journey, and others may come to a conclusion different from mine. It is the journey itself, the honest evaluation of objectives for Isle Royale and the weighing of values, that I hope each reader of this book will undertake.

It is appropriate to state that my scientific career is not dependent on the wolves' existence. I could address problems on the island without wolves. As a scientist, however, it has been my professional preoccupation to explore the role of wolves in nature, and Isle Royale happens to be one of the best places on the planet to do this. Perhaps I am handicapped by a fascination with the wolves; I care deeply about their future, for I have learned that these animals help sustain life as we know it on Isle Royale.

In the spring of 1988, our immediate concerns took precedence over long-term considerations. Within five days Bob and I were handling wolves—gambling with the crown jewels, as it were. Over the next several years, almost every wolf alive on the island in 1988 was weighed, measured, examined, blood-sampled for disease and genetic studies, radiocollared, and then promptly sent on its way. Much new knowledge was revealed by the more intensive study, and no wolves were sacrificed in the process. During this period, I concentrated my efforts on gathering data, expecting that the new information would produce a better vista for making management recommendations.

We learned that a suspected pathogen, canine parvovirus (CPV), had indeed invaded the island, but then died out. Its occurrence corresponded exactly to the wolf crash of 1980 to 1982, and to the chronic high mortality of 1982 to 1988. As an invisible agent of death for dogs both domestic and wild, CPV was carried inadvertently to Isle Royale, and to every other corner of the world, by people. All evidence, circumstantial though it was, pointed to CPV as the cause of the dramatic wolf decline and the high mortality of the 1980s.

Antibodies to CPV in the wolves' blood disappeared after 1988, but during the rest of their lives the surviving wolves usually failed to reproduce at normal rates. CPV was gone, so something else must explain the poor reproduction in Isle Royale's wolves. Food shortage did not seem to be an important factor, as the number of old moose present in 1990 was identical to the level of the 1970s, when twice as many wolves were present. Genetic losses remained a possible cause of their troubles, perhaps producing inbreeding depression, or poor early survival. However, we actually know little about the significance of lost genetic variability in isolated populations living in the wild.

Molecular studies confirmed the worst-case genetic scenario for Isle Royale wolves—they were heavily inbred. The high death toll of the 1980s,

After four decades of total freedom, wolves on Isle Royale have been live-trapped and radiocollared after a close examination to determine exposure to disease and take genetic sampling.

linked to an introduced disease, had produced such a low point in wolf numbers that random events alone could easily snuff them out. Rapid genetic decay brought on by the passage of many generations might accentuate the risks. Scientific dogma and raw probability seemed to predict the demise of the wolves, and each year of poor reproduction was another nail in their collective coffin. Years went by, and the wolves failed to recover.

By 1993 the wolf population was top-heavy with old animals that seemed unable to replace themselves. Only three females, all quite old, were known to exist among the 13 wolves left, and only one of these had ever successfully reared young. But in the same year two of these females, in adjacent packs, reared four pups each—a normal litter size. This surprising change dramatically improved the odds of survival for the wolf population. A new generation had finally materialized, ready to take over when the parents succumbed to old age. Indeed, less than a year after we discovered the eight new pups, three of the four parents died.

Meanwhile, incriminating evidence from other areas linked CPV to the population dynamics of wild wolves. Historical analysis by Dave Mech showed that the ebb and flow of wolf numbers in northern Minnesota was correlated with exposure to CPV. In 1994, a wild wolf collared by Mech died from this disease.

In the same year, as evidence mounted that disease, not food shortage, had caused the wolf crash on Isle Royale in the previous decade, the NPS offered vaccination against parvovirus as an allowable intervention. After soliciting expert advice, I declined to vaccinate the wolves. Our goal, remember, had less to do with saving the current population than with learning as much as we could about the real-world dangers faced by a small population of wolves. We had completely missed the initial parvovirus outbreak, but now, remarkably, Isle Royale was parvo-free. Antibodies to CPV in the wolves themselves were our best indicator of disease exposure. Vaccination, which uses a modified version of the live virus to stimulate protective antibodies, would also make it impossible to determine whether CPV itself was present. The opportunity to learn more about disease risks outweighed other options, and with the concurrence of the NPS, I chose to leave the wolves untreated and unprotected.

The decision not to vaccinate was made for scientific reasons, but I sensed later that I had inadvertently assisted the NPS down a slippery slope of nonintervention. Passive observation can be an easy policy that doesn't require much expense or ecological understanding; perhaps that explains some of its appeal. But our national parks deserve better than rote adherence to tradition.

In the mid-1990s, with new data compiled, it is time to examine rigorously the policy options available to the NPS regarding the future of wolves on Isle Royale. As Winston Churchill once quipped, "At times it becomes necessary to do what is required." Managers could continue a hands-off tradition, allowing the wolves to die out and, should that occur, waiting for wolves to return on their own. If this is the inclination of Park Service managers, however, it should be stated openly and supported by scientific and aesthetic arguments, and the public should have a chance to voice its opinion.

As we consider the future of Isle Royale's wolves, we should think of our national parks as both laboratories and cathedrals[2]. There is genuine creative tension between science and soul, reason and myth. It is appropriate to celebrate this tension in our national parks, not to bury it in administrative rules or stale traditions. The wolves of Isle Royale have served both science and the human spirit for many years—ask any visitor. Science simply illuminates in a modest way that which invigorates the human soul. Let no park manager (or scientist) forget the importance of the latter!

Shelved in the headquarters of every national park are thick three-ring binders containing the "Management Policies of the National Park Service." After reading these tomes it would seem, on the surface at least, that the NPS is well-prepared to meet any challenge of the twenty-first century. However, the subtle yet serious problems our parks now face cannot be solved without thoughtful attention and creative action.

In recent decades, NPS management has been influenced by a certain worldview, an expedient myth that summarizes a twentieth-century view of nature first developed in North America by descendants of European immigrants. Simply stated, it says "nature knows best," assuming that "nature" includes all life and processes apart from humans. Whenever humans run roughshod over the rest of nature, problems occur; one can learn more of this from Chief Seattle, Aldo Leopold, Rachel Carson, and dozens of later writers. However, leaving humanity out of nature is simply naive. Absolute wilderness (where the effects of humans are absent) is a myth; human influence pervades every corner of the earth. Natural events at Isle Royale in the last half of the twentieth century have helped reinforce a noninterventionist policy of management within the NPS, but the limitations of this approach may become most clear at Isle Royale. Perhaps here, the human animal can find its proper place. In the words of Paul Tillich, "Mankind becomes really human only at the time of decision."

For over four decades, Isle Royale embodied the notion of the forest primeval, a world in ecological equilibrium—that beautiful and elusive "balance of nature." This balance was effected most readily in "absolute wilderness," in the complete absence of human direction. For decades, people said, "After all, look at Isle Royale."

Isle Royale's forests, flowers, and wildlife are a national treasure. All citizens have a stake in its future and a responsibility to guide its management.

Hiking trails on Isle Royale are lined with wildflowers. In June these Canada dogwoods (bunchberries) are in flower; the red fruit appears in mid-July.

Common in early summer, tiger swallowtails extract
nutrients from many sources, including wolf scat,
rotting carcasses, and mineral springs.

Though lovely to look at, the Amanita mushroom
is quite poisonous for people. Red squirrels, on the
other hand, relish this mushroom in August.

The hands-off philosophy that directed the prevailing NPS management notion fit hand in glove with a powerful idea in Western civilization—that the human species is distinct from other forms of "lower" animal life, that we have somehow risen above nature, that nature will operate properly only if we are kept out of the picture. It is an old idea that can be traced back to treatises by Greek and Roman scholars. But it is a perception that ecologist Daniel Botkin believes to be "one of the main impediments to progress on environmental issues."[3] The view that modern humans have no legitimate role as players in the "natural" world of wilderness is a pervasive one. I understand it, and I have sympathized with it in some instances. But in fact, we are natural creatures rooted in the earth, and it is by our unique mental capacities that "nature" and "natural" are defined. Ralph Waldo Emerson considered nature to be the "shadow of man," and Loren Eiseley felt that "no word bears a heavier, or more ancient, or more diverse array of meanings."

In his book *Discordant Harmony*, Botkin states that we must recognize that humans already play a role in every ecosystem on earth, and that we have the capacity and insight to intervene softly on behalf of all life. He argues that the smaller the size of a "natural" area, the greater the need for human involvement to maintain important ecological processes. We must mitigate for the constrictions we have already imposed on nature.

With the laboratory and cathedral metaphor in mind, let us look for guidance from the management policies of the NPS. In our national parks, for example, there is a clear dictate to favor the conservation of native species, as opposed to those that arrived with the assistance of humans. Native species belong to the primeval communities present before European civilization arrived to mess things up. However, one must deal with the surprising fact that moose were evidently not present on Isle Royale prior to the twentieth century. Both the absence of moose on the island in the nineteenth century and the increased numbers of moose in northern Ontario, which precipitated their arrival on Isle Royale, had everything to do with the spread of European civilization. Europeans first provided firearms to native humans, then virtually eliminated the natives and logged and burned vast regions, creating favorable conditions for moose.

Careful archaeological work by the NPS has revealed much evidence over the past 4,000 years of Native Americans, caribou, and beaver on Isle

Royale, but no indication that moose or wolves inhabited Isle Royale before 1900. Thus the NPS policy of maintaining "native" species cannot clearly guide us in our current quandary. In an ironic blend of tradition and history, one might argue that neither the wolf nor the moose are purely "native" species at Isle Royale.

Another NPS management policy states that natural processes will be relied upon as much as possible to regulate wildlife populations. At Isle Royale, it is abundantly clear that wolf predation has helped control the moose population, thereby influencing the entire forest community. One can actually find indirect evidence of the influence of wolves in growth rings of the island's trees[4]. Wolf predation certainly qualifies as an important natural process that could be maintained, according to policy. However, is not extinction also a natural process? Animal populations on islands are naturally prone to wild swings and high rates of extinction. There is a large element of chance in the makeup of an island's fauna because of the limited number of species. Should we favor predation, or species extinction? NPS policy does not tell us which natural process should take precedence.

If wolves were extirpated naturally and no human causation was detected, could they also return naturally, or has human activity altered the recolonization possibilities for wolves? This is a relatively easy question to answer, as there are 100,000 people in the city of Thunder Bay on the mainland shore. The city comes complete with its network of highways and rail lines, which reduce the likelihood that wolves would inhabit the shoreline and make the run to Isle Royale.

That run to the island, of course, *must* be done in winter, across the ice of Lake Superior. Given the long-term prospect of global warming, can we really assume that ice will form on Lake Superior with a "natural" frequency? Throughout the warm decade of the 1980s, which followed a decades-long warming trend, there were almost no ice bridges from Isle Royale to the mainland. There is a broad (but by no means unanimous) scientific opinion that the warming of the global environment can be attributed to the build-up of CO_2 and other greenhouse gases, resulting from the combustion of fossil fuels. Must we be able to assess the uncertainties involved in the historic warming of the entire northern hemisphere before we decide whether wolves have a future on Isle Royale?

The warming trend in the northern hemisphere
has left Isle Royale without an ice bridge to the
mainland during most winters.

The more one is drawn into this question, the more convoluted the answers become.

In one area, at least, NPS policy would seem to provide a clear path. NPS management recognizes the need to eliminate exotic species, and to mitigate past human disturbance. This is an enlightened view, for exotic organisms transported by humans around the earth have been responsible for most species extinctions in recorded history.

In the case of invisible disease organisms, although there is no practical way to wall off the parks, it will sometimes be possible to mitigate after the fact. In view of the strong circumstantial evidence linking the collapse of the wolf population from 1980 to 1982 (and the decline thereafter) to an introduced disease, it seems legitimate to restore the wolves after the mayhem passes. Yet the National Park Service has not faced this particular combination of circumstances elsewhere, and it is understandably reluctant to step in.

When the advice of Fraser Darling, a noted wildlife scientist, was sought concerning elephant "overpopulation" in Kenya's Tsavo National Park, he responded that, "The surest road to the right answer usually lies

The cause of naturally ignited fires on Isle Royale, lightning is a common occurrence in summer. Within certain constraints, the National Park Service now allows such fires to burn unimpeded.

This lightning-induced fire burned along a ridgetop for several weeks in 1988, but it could not move into the green forest off the ridge.

along a simple path uncovered by common sense." Yet E.O. Wilson, also a noted scientist, considered common sense to be "that overrated capacity composed of the set of prejudices we acquire by the age of 18."

Common sense may imply an appeal to mass opinion, which could be ill-advised when applied to the little-understood complexity of nature within our national parks. I prefer to use the term "ecological realism" as a guideline, under which options are laid out based on our best understanding of ecological relationships. In that vein, we can assume that moose are likely to be part of the fauna that inhabit Isle Royale National Park for the foreseeable future—for at least another century. We have already seen that wolves have reduced moose density for long periods of time, enabling plant communities to develop that would not even appear if moose population growth was unchecked by wolves. There can be no natural process more closely aligned with the behavior and evolution of moose than wolf predation, that inscrutable agent of natural selection.

Moose are what they are due to eons of close shepherding by wolves. In the words of the poet Robinson Jeffers,

> What but the wolf's tooth whittled so fine
> The fleet limbs of the antelope.

It seems only prudent to maintain wolf predation on Isle Royale as long as moose continue to inhabit the place. No one can say how long that might be; over the span of centuries, few things in nature are permanent. According to the Roman poet Lucretius, writing in the first century B.C., "not one thing is like itself forever."

Adherence to policy directives or appeals to common sense do not address all the values at stake at Isle Royale. The unique characteristics of this park demand specific consideration, and both science and soul should be part of the formula.

In the 1990s, at the urging of the National Academy of Sciences, the NPS began to prepare a new vision—one that included an explicit role for science in the management of our parks. The motto "Science for parks, and parks for science" was bandied about, and there were calls for institutional change. These ideas were reminiscent of those expressed 30 years before in the 1963 Leopold Report, which reviewed the role of science in national park management: "We recommend that the NPS recognize the enormous complexity of ecologic communities and the diversity of management procedures required to preserve them."[5]

A similar recommendation was made by an earlier National Academy of Sciences report, which was also released in 1963. According to more than a dozen additional official reviews issued since that time, an absence of adequate science and monitoring to ensure long-term ecological integrity will reduce national parks to scenic pleasuring grounds with an uncertain future.

Allowing nature free rein in national parks is not as easy as one might suppose, even when the effort is backed by good science and determination. One scientific success within our national parks involved demonstrating the essential role that fire plays in maintaining diverse types of forest communities. Because of this new understanding, the rigid fire suppression programs that had been part of park management since the NPS was established were slowly relaxed in the 1970s.

But nature dishes out extremes on a grand scale, as the world discovered during the Yellowstone fires of 1988. Such large natural processes are not easily accommodated in and around most national parks, regardless of policy. Before the smoke had cleared, the U.S. Congress demanded a thorough review of fire management in national parks. For the next five years, until Isle Royale National Park produced a revised fire management plan that had been signed off at all levels of the bureaucracy, all lightning-started fires were suppressed on the island.

As fate would have it, a single dry thunderstorm in August of 1991 started four fires on Isle Royale in one evening, something I had not observed in the previous two decades. If they had not been extinguished by fire crews, these fires might have profoundly changed the character of the island. We will never know. A former Interior Department official sent a brief note acknowledging this news in my annual report, volunteering that it was "unconscionable" for the NPS to put out natural fires on Isle Royale. After 1993, with an approved fire management plan on line, lightning-started fires were once again allowed to burn, under prescribed conditions. The catch? It may be more expensive to allow a fire to burn naturally than to extinguish it, because of the demanding monitoring schedule stimulated by Congressional demands. So it goes.

As a tool, science is moot on the question of whether wolves belong aboard the Isle Royale ark. Yet science has given us a glimpse of what we might expect in their absence. The wolf reduction of the 1980s illustrated how wolf predation had previously kept moose in check and allowed the forest to grow. In the complete absence of wolves, moose might so destroy their own resource base that they would face extinction themselves. This almost happened to reindeer on St. Matthew, a tundra island in the Bering Sea.

At Isle Royale, where plant life is much more productive, it is likely that moose would, through a series of increases and crashes, simply dig in for the long haul. The successful moose would be those that were adapted to extreme resource scarcity. This adaptation is accomplished by growing to a smaller size, with a correspondingly smaller demand for resources. Such developments are evident in island fauna scattered across the earth— caribou on the Slate Islands in Lake Superior, black-tailed deer on Alaska's Coronation Island, red deer on the island of Rhum off the coast of Great Britain and, in the southern hemisphere, reindeer on the island of St. Georgia. An extreme example, a truly miniaturized elephant only a few feet tall, existed on several Mediterranean islands during the Pleistocene. Striking fossil evidence from red deer on the British island of Jersey, off the coast of present-day France, indicates that such miniaturization might be accomplished in as little as 6,000 years—a mere 2,000 generations[6].

The scientific value of allowing Isle Royale to remain wolfless would involve the study of a runaway population of large herbivores and its effects on plants. How high would the moose population go with only starvation to stop them? What particular combination of physical deterioration and severe winter weather would precede moose die offs? How much would annual production of calves be reduced as moose density increases? What new direction might the plant community and all other life take in the absence of a top carnivore? Better answers would be possible now than could be obtained in the 1930s, when all this happened before, because our tools have improved. However, general answers to these questions are already available from other areas.

The frequency of wolf recolonization and extinction in the absence of human interference is possibly of scientific interest. The mechanics of extinction for small populations are certainly important to understand, and this quest explains the consensus that allowed the wolf population to flounder in the late 1980s. In the event of extinction, the schedule for

Such a rare bull moose with misshapen antlers was sometimes called a "Windigo" (Wee-tee-go in Cree is the evil spirit that devours mankind). The animal was probably a reproductively senile bull moose with inadequate testosterone, or an accidental castrate.

wolf reappearance would depend on human development on the mainland, ice cover on Lake Superior, and the dispersal idiosyncrasies of wolves inhabiting the mainland shore—all circumstances unique to Isle Royale. Larger questions of broad scientific interest would be unapproachable.

I believe we stand to gain more, scientifically, by furthering the existence of wolves on Isle Royale, and by propping them up when necessary. A minimal maintenance program would probably suffice, as a recent mathematical simulation suggests that the mean time before extinction for small, isolated wolf populations is at least several decades. One important question to explore is the robustness or repeatability of the wolf-moose relationship at Isle Royale. When wolves entered the scene in the late 1940s, moose were evidently at a very low level. Could wolves also successfully regulate an overpopulation of moose? Could an infusion of new genes from mainland wolves perk up a wolf population suffering from genetic isolation and inbreeding? What about the long-term dynamics of wolf and moose populations? Population fluctuations must occur on a time scale of decades for such long-lived animals, and there is no other locale known where the nature of their fluctuations is likely to be discovered.

Scientific value aside, however, the most influential arguments regarding the future of any national park will be spiritual, or inspirational. The Hubble telescope project had support from the public because people were inspired by the prospect of visible images from the edge of the universe, not by millions of bits of data stored in the computer banks of scientists. While the scientific perspective can be distilled to black and white choices, more subjective values have legitimate appeal.

Spirit is a powerful influence in the management of national parks and wilderness. For many wilderness advocates, an island left to the devices of nature, not overrun by technological humans, conjures up powerful images. For some people, even well-intentioned human intervention may degrade a wilderness. Isolated in a tempestuous lake, little visited by humans (by NPS standards), closed in winter, and replete with large carnivores as well as their prey, Isle Royale has clearly been left to nature, not man. Who would care to change that?

The wolf is more than simply a member of the Isle Royale fauna. Ecologically, it plays a disproportionately important role as a top carnivore. More significantly, the wolf is the enabler of a successful marriage between cathedral and laboratory. It is an important image—one that allowed Isle Royale management to escape the angst and attention associated with other national parks, where natural areas have been more significantly compromised by the ills of modern civilization. Since the wolves arrived, the NPS has been in an enviable position at Isle Royale, because the island's fauna and flora got along rather nicely without human help. A very capable park superintendent once confided to me that his biggest management challenge at Isle Royale was directing his own staff.

In avoiding the bumpy road that other parks have been forced to follow, Isle Royale has stimulated major advances in public understanding of natural areas. In 1931, when Isle Royale was designated a national park, the NPS itself was less than 20 years old. The 1916 legislation that established the agency set forth a vision for our national parks that has undergone little change in the decades that followed:

". . . to conserve the scenery and the natural and historic objects and the wildlife therein, and to provide for the enjoyment of the same in such manner and by such means as will leave them unimpaired for the enjoyment of future generations."

Early parks were opened up as attractive recreation areas and managed as facades of scenery, with little or no understanding of their ecological underpinnings. Because of the utilitarian attitudes of early twentieth-century Americans, wolves and mountain lions were eliminated to protect game animals, bears were fed in public sideshows, laundry operations were set up in natural hot springs, and resorts were placed in the middle of key natural features. Society is still paying dearly for some of these early mistakes.

In 1929, as momentum grew to create a national park at Isle Royale, the Michigan state legislature funded a study of the island's natural resources and archaeology. The $15,000 dedicated to this task may be, in constant dollars, the greatest single financial commitment ever made to study the resources of Isle Royale.

Enter Adolph Murie, a wildlife biologist with a new Ph.D degree, who came to Isle Royale in the summers of 1929 and 1930 in order to study its fauna. Murie would eventually conduct the first scientific study of wolves in Alaska's Mt. McKinley National Park; at Isle Royale, he launched what became one of the first studies of moose conducted anywhere.

After two to three decades of unrestricted growth, the moose population at Isle Royale had reached an unheard of density in the late 1920s, and Murie concluded that both the ecosystem and the moose were suffering. Murie was a staunch preservationist whose wilderness vision for Isle Royale was extreme, but he nonetheless felt that the runaway moose population had to be limited through human action. He recommended a moose reduction through public hunting, state-authorized shooting, live-trapping and removal, or the introduction of large carnivores such as wolves. The "land should not be teeming only with moose," Murie wrote, "but teeming with all of nature."[7] Such holistic thinking was atypical within the national parks of the 1930s, but it was a hallmark of

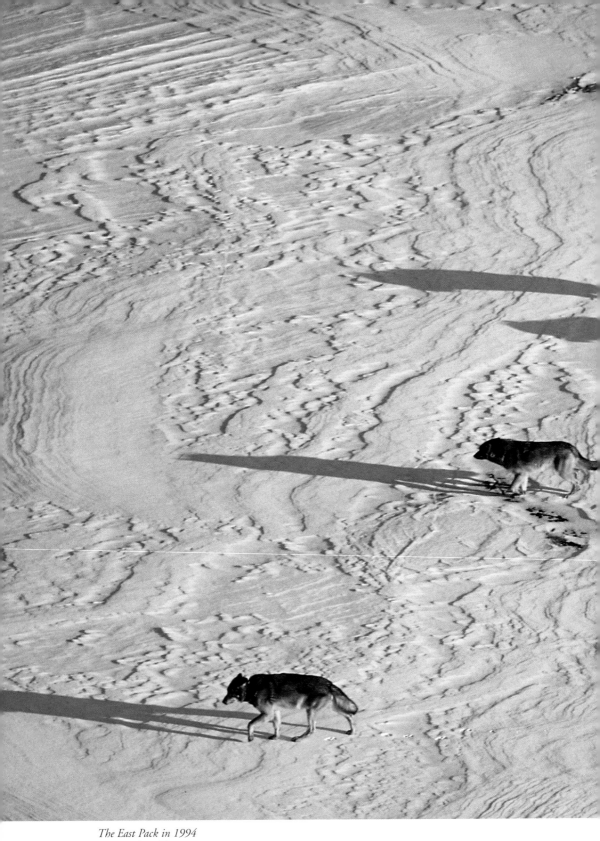

The East Pack in 1994
begins a day of hunting.

philosophy for Adolph Murie and his older brother Olaus, a wildlife biologist who gained prominence for his studies of park wildlife and his advocacy of wilderness.

When Murie's study and recommendations were finally published, after a several-year delay caused by lack of funding, Isle Royale was mostly public land in limbo. Its national park status had been approved by Congress in 1931, but there was no money appropriated for land acquisition. Through most of the 1930s, the island was owned primarily by the state of Michigan, a custodian whose interest waned as full park status slowly became a reality. Murie's recommendations sat on the shelf, and his prediction of an inevitable die off of moose was realized in 1934. Later, the Michigan Department of Conservation arranged to move 71 moose by boat from Isle Royale to the mainland, hoping to relieve population pressures and reestablish moose on the mainland. It was a heroic effort, but of no consequence to the island's huge moose population.

In 1936 Adolph Murie took a job with the NPS, directing Civilian Conservation Corps projects in western parks. He was asked to summarize his vision for managing Isle Royale as a national park. His comments were direct and uncompromising when it came to the wilderness potential of the island. Wilderness was, he felt, the greatest value of the park. In Murie's view, the park should not be developed as a popular summer resort; he even argued against the establishment of a system of hiking trails. He felt the NPS should "secure personnel which has a feeling for wilderness and an understanding of wilderness values".[7]

Murie would probably have considered the term "wilderness management" an oxymoron. He suggested advising NPS administrators that their success depended not on "projects accomplished, but by projects sidetracked." Such candor in official reports was rare, even in those days. In the same year Adolph's brother Olaus, together with the likes of Robert Marshall and Aldo Leopold, formed the Wilderness Society, an organization dedicated to the preservation of wilderness.

The NPS took a more traditional tack than the one recommended by Murie, allowing some development and suppressing "unsightly" natural fires. Wildfires that began in logging slash had raged through the island in 1936. Nevertheless, the wilderness character of Isle Royale was an influential ideal, unique among national parks of the day.

After the "catastrophic" moose decline during the spring die off of 1934 and perhaps additional declines after the fire of 1936, moose numbers rebounded in the 1940s. Another biologist, the U.S. Fish and Wildlife Service's Laurits Krefting, sounded an alarm by calling for moose controls—either via the gun or through introduction of a large carnivore such as the wolf. The "moose question" at Isle Royale was again a major issue. The NPS response was another study, conducted this time by James Cole, a Park Service biologist. Cole reported that winter browse was abundant, and believed the moose population needed no public assistance. The Park Service encouraged private efforts to release wolves on Isle Royale in 1952, as a partial solution to the concerns over moose numbers, but this failed when wolves released from the Detroit Zoo proved to be too tame. In any case, wild wolves got there first, and the rest is history.

By the 1960s, when the NPS began to undertake the challenge of managing living landscapes, Isle Royale was widely recognized as an ecosystem with all of its parts intact. Historian Al Runte claimed that among national parks, Isle Royale "had come closest to the ideal ecological preserve."[8] No one can take much credit for this; it emerged from the geography of the park. The presence of wolves completed a classic food chain, inspiring a scientific quest and helping to rehabilitate the wolf's reputation in the mind of the public. The "bloodthirsty demon" became a saint in the wilderness.

I sense a rocky road for the NPS should it select, unilaterally or with rudimentary review, a hands-off option for management of wolves on Isle Royale. The interested public—the real constituency of our national parks—is well-educated and supportive of complete ecosystems. For the past three decades, through its interpretive programs and materials for public education, the Park Service has passed along research findings that demonstrate the vital role of wolf predation in the ecology of Isle Royale. Most visitors to the park have heard of the boom and bust pattern of the moose population that prevailed before the arrival of wolves. It was a true story and a good one, and the public accepted it.

If wolves are to be excluded on the grounds that it would be unnatural to bring them back, then it would seem that the interpretive message has been wrong all these years. Perhaps the significant aspect of the wolves on Isle Royale was not their creative importance as an evolutionary force, not their health and welfare program for moose, not their indirect role in maintaining plant life that would otherwise be diminished, not their symbolic importance to the wilderness aura of Isle Royale. Instead, the salient feature of Isle Royale wolves—what really mattered—was simply their method of arrival. Perhaps NPS interpreters could get that message across to a perplexed public, but I could not.

In an earlier era that we both knew, Durward Allen wrote, "The moose and wolf need no one to lead them . . . only a place to be left alone."[9] Isle Royale has been that place for 40 years, serving as both cathedral and laboratory. But of what use is a cathedral without sacred imagery? Of what value is a laboratory without subjects?

If wolves are to be assured a future on Isle Royale, their greatest sanctuary, Park Service managers must courageously face their toughest resource management decision—one that will set a precedent for other parks and wilderness areas. It is a question to be embraced, not avoided. If the wolves of Isle Royale are threatened by insularity, can the grizzlies of Yellowstone be far behind? Enlightened by 35 years of scientific research and sensitive to an informed public, humans have a magnificent opportunity to use intellect in sustaining nature. The risk is not great, and there will always be opportunities—perhaps once or twice a century—to reverse the decision.

Someday, when I am long gone, animal and plant life on Isle Royale may be so changed that wisdom will call for a different approach. But this time around, at the dawn of a new millennium, I must vote for the wolves.

NOTES

[1]Peterson, R. O. and R. J. Krumenaker. 1989. "Wolf Decline on Isle Royale: A Biological and Policy Conundrum." The George Wright Forum 6:10-15.

[2]For these metaphors I am indebted to Tom McNamee (1987). *Nature First.* Roberts Rinehart, Inc. Boulder, CO. 54pp.

[3]Pages 8, 91, and 124 in Botkin, D. B. 1990. *Discordant Harmonies.* Oxford University Press. 241pp.

[4]McLaren and Peterson, 1994. *Science* 266: 1555-1558.

[5]Leopold, A. S., S. A. Cain, C. M. Cottam, I. N. Gabrielson, and T. L. Kimball. 1963. "Wildlife Management in the National Parks." Trans. N. Amer. Wildl. and Natur. Resour. Conf. 28:28-45.

[6]Lister, A. 1994. *Natural History* 6/94: 60-61.

[7]Little, John J. 1980. "Adolph Murie and the Wilderness Ideal for Isle Royale National Park." Pages 97-114 in Lora, Ronald (ed.). The American West: Essays in Honor of W. Eugene Hollan. University of Toledo, Toledo, Ohio.

[8]Page 147 in Runte, A. 1987. *National Parks, the American Experience.* University of Nebraska Press, Lincoln, NB. 335pp.

[9]Allen, D. L. 1979. *Wolves of Minong.* Houghton Mifflin Co., Boston. 499pp.

ADDITIONAL SOURCES

Eiseley, Loren. 1987. In Kenneth Heuer, *The Lost Notebooks of Loren Eiseley.* Little, Brown and Co., Boston.

Steinhart, Peter. "Dreaming Elands." In Robert Finch and John Elder, eds., *The Norton Book of Nature Writing.* W.W. Norton, New York.

Allen, Durward L. *Wolves of Minong.* The University of Michigan Press, Ann Arbor, Michigan.